Empirical Sexual Attitudes

Science's best answers to hard questions about psychology and sexuality

Kodi B. Arfer

Contents

Why do strange, apparently useless sexual taboos appear in all human societies? Experiments show that people associate sexuality with animals and the body, and thus with mortality. It appears that social norms ranging from disapproval of prostitution to the ideal of romantic love exist, in part, to provide us a kind of symbolic immortality and buffer us from existential threat. There exist other potential explanations for sexual taboos, but the overall picture is not favorable to anyone who would seek to free human sexuality from artificial restrictions.

Experiments have demonstrated a wide variety of ways sexual emotion can influence how we think and decide. Importantly, such findings have been obtained even for non-sexual domains of behavior, and with very weak manipulations of sexual affect, such as the gender of a name. Sexuality then appears to have pervasive, albeit subtle, consequences for human thought. There is no clear overall theme to the findings, except, perhaps, that sexuality often influences us in ways we'd rather not be influenced.

Sexual activity to which one partner does not consent is seen in all human cultures and many non-human species. Its frequency can differ dramatically between cultures, but it is very common in the United States, especially between acquaintances and romantic partners and in its milder forms. Rape is associated with even more psychological damage to the victim than non-sexual traumas, and even sexual abuse short of rape is damaging. The evidence of damage from child sexual abuse, however, is less clear than the evidence of damage from abuse of adults. Precisely what makes sexual abuse aversive during the event and traumatizing afterwards is unclear.

The idea that sexual abuse is an act of desperation by sexually deprived men is not supported. However, sexual abuse does seem to be motivated by sexual interest in the victim and by less selective sexual preferences (specifically, a tendency not to be sexually inhibited by expressions of non-consent). In terms of non-sexual causes, abuse seems to share the causes of non-sexual crimes and antisocial behavior, and it is enabled by cultural environments in which women are less powerful and by sexist attitudes. What all this means for prevention and treatment is unclear.

Preface

I introduce the goal of this book—to determine what sexual attitudes we should endorse if we want our attitudes to be as faithful as possible to the available empirical evidence—and provide some background.

As long as sex is dealt with in the current confusion of ignorance and sophistication, denial and indulgence, suppression and stimulation, punishment and exploitation, secrecy and display, it will be associated with a duplicity and indecency that lead neither to intellectual honesty nor human dignity. [Gregg, 1948, p. v]

Historically and to this day, people have had strong opinions about sex. Religions have praised some sexual behaviors as spiritually productive while condemning others as contrary to divine plans. Physicians, since the Victorian era, have offered a similar range of commandments, from branding masturbation as self-abuse to warning against the perils of sexual repression. And laypeople of all kinds have opined, sometimes in yet more emphatic terms, as to what kinds of sexual expression or abstinence are virtuous, disgusting, immoral, unnatural, innocent, beautiful, heroic, unthinkable, satisfying, worthwhile, dangerous, or stupid.

The only thing that such opinions can defensibly be founded on is the one thing they're least likely to be founded on: empirical evidence. Think about it: in the twenty-first century, it's no secret that human intuition about the way the universe works is wrong. We aren't born knowing that the earth orbits the sun, bananas gravitationally attract other objects, microorganisms live under our skin, and the best choice in the Monty Hall problem is to switch.[1] Our own behavior is no different. As much as we observe and reason about each other in everyday life, experimental psychology has shown time and again that human behavior and cognition can be nothing like what we expect. The ultimate demonstration is Nisbett and Wilson (1977), which shows through converging evidence that despite a persistent intuition to the contrary, people do not have special introspective access to the causes of their own behavior. The paper is thus a defense of the necessity of experimental psychology by means of experimental psychology itself.

[1] The Monty Hall problem is a math problem with a famously counterintuitive answer. Suppose you're a contestant on a game show and there are three doors, one of which has a car behind it, whereas each of other two doors has only a goat behind it. The car and the goats are assigned to the doors at random, with each possibility being equally likely. You may choose any door without opening it, and then the host will open a door that you *didn't* choose to reveal a goat. (If your initially chosen door had the car, the host has two goat doors to select, and will select one at random. If your initially chosen door had a goat, there is only one other door with a goat, so the host will open that door.) Now the host lets you either open the door you first picked, or open the remaining unopened door. Are you more likely to get the car if you stay or switch? It turns out that your chance of getting the car is 1/3 if you stay but 2/3 if you switch. See the Wikipedia article "Monty Hall problem" for a full discussion.

Unfortunately, experimental psychology hasn't filtered down to the lay public. This problem isn't confined to psychology: a typical person doesn't even understand the falsificatory scientific method to begin with, any more than they realize that pure mathematics concerns proof rather than computation. But it seems all the more galling in the case of psychology. Whereas research-level mathematics is rarely directly relevant to everyday life, we rely on our own ideas of how people think and behave all the time: our decisions are (or at least, should be) based on what we expect the consequences of our actions will be for others' and our own behavior. Incorrect expectations will thus lead to incorrect decisions.

In the case of sexuality, things only get worse. We tend to have strong opinions, not mere intuitions, and sexual attitudes can be surprisingly high-stakes considering how sexual matters are sometimes dismissed as trivial. Think of STDs, unwanted pregnancies, rape, and violence against gay men and lesbians. Or, just notice how people's decisions about whom to marry and how much to reproduce play a major role in determining the course of their lives. Perhaps most importantly of all, sexual motivation can have consequences for behavior that seemingly has nothing to do with sex, as discussed in this book's chapter on cognition. You may not agree that these are all issues of sexuality per se. Fair enough. For the purposes of this book, let's just take "sexuality" to refer to the set of emotions and motivations that seem closely tied to sex and masturbation, where "sex" includes (now and hereinafter) coitus, oral sex, anal sex, and so on. How sexuality thus defined relates to rape etc. is an empirical matter, one of the several empirical matters that I hope to shed light on in the course of this book.

As disparate as the topics I'll discuss may seem to be, I have a single overarching goal: to provide a foundation for empirical sexual attitudes. I've just complained about how sexual attitudes tend not to have much to do with empirical truth, and how sexual attitudes can ultimately matter a lot. What I want to do, then, is try to junk all our accumulated, entangled ideas about what sexuality is or ought to be and replace them with notions that are as faithful as possible to the available evidence.

That evidence isn't nearly as good as it could be. Sexuality isn't the most popular of research topics. And studies that do concern sexuality are rarely true experiments—that is, studies in which subjects are randomly assigned to experimental conditions, which are the only sort of study that provides direct evidence of causation. Non-experimental research, in which subjects are only observed without being manipulated by the researcher, or are manipulated but without true random assignment, predominates. Why is this so? Partly because of theoretical and practical difficulties inherent in manipulating relevant variables (such as sexual experience) and partly because of antagonism that some clinical psychologists, psychiatrists, sociologists, and anthropologists have towards the artificiality of the lab.

Worst of all, a large part of academic research on sexuality is not empirical. It eschews the scientific method in favor of the critical method, replacing repeatable procedures and numerical measurement with anything-goes interpretation. Society has somehow chosen writers like Sigmund Freud, Michel Foucault, bell hooks, and Judith Butler to represent academia's opinions on sexual matters. All this noise masks the important gaps in empirical sex research. So, I have a limited supply of raw material—empirical truth—with which to construct this book, but I'll do the best I can.

On the subject of this book's limitations, let me say a bit about where I'm coming from and what my biases are. Unlike virtually every other academic who writes about sex these days, I'm more sex-negative than sex-positive. Although raised by atheist parents with reasonably liberal attitudes about sex, I developed a very dim view of human sexuality during puberty. My views have mellowed since then, but I remain celibate, and my scientific interest in sexuality has its roots in my fear and distrust of these strange and powerful motivational forces.

As for my qualifications, my formal education is exclusively in psychology and mathematics. I've learned some other things on my own, but for some of the disciplines touched on this book, including psychiatry, ethology, anthropology, criminology, and history, what I've read hardly extends beyond what I've cited here. Please let me know of any errors or omissions.

Finally, a few words on feminism. I am sympathetic to feminism, but more to the second-wave, radical feminism of the early 1970s than the third-wave, sex-positive feminism that is popular today. Insofar as sex-positivity is the assumption that human sexuality is intrinsically good and thus any way in which sexuality seems to have bad consequences (such as rape) doesn't count as sexuality (along the lines of "no true Scotsman"), sex-positivity is dogmatic. And I see it as less important to assert women's femininity and unity than their personhood and individuality, as Haack (2001) describes, and as opposed to what Echols (1989) calls "cultural feminism". I would like not to equalize gender roles but to abolish them. To borrow some rhetoric from the *Brown v. Board of Education* decision, there is no "separate but equal": separate is inherently unequal. In any case, various points of feminist thinking, second-wave and otherwise, will be among the things we examine from an empirical point of view in this book.

Acknowledgments

Thanks to (in alphabetical order) Jeffrey H. Arfer, Nicholas R. Eaton, Gambit Garrison, Edvard Karlsen, prude, Leianne Stafford, and Elizabeth M. Trimber for their thoughtful comments on various drafts of this book and the productive discussions I had with them.

Diversity of sexual practices is not bad

There is currently no empirical basis for condemning most sexual practices, as strange or disgusting as people may find them. Nor is there any empirical basis for condemning sexual abstinence: in particular, there is at best weak support for the idea of a hunger-like sex drive. Clinical trials of sexual behavior would be necessary to begin shedding light on the issue of what sexual habits are most beneficial.

Contents

Sexual indulgence

The word "sex" often refers specifically to coitus (penile–vaginal intercourse), but various other activities are usually also considered sex, such as anal sex, fellatio, cunnilingus, and mutual masturbation. Sex is typically between two people, but then there's group sex. Typically the participants are of opposite sexes, but sometimes they aren't. Often the participants are roughly the same age and consider themselves to be in a passionate and intimate relationship although they aren't related by blood, but sometimes they're of vastly different ages or they don't even know each others' names or they're siblings. Usually sex is consensual, but sometimes it isn't: a party who doesn't really want to have sex has somehow been coerced into it. And if one of the participants is human, then usually they all are, but sometimes animals are included as well. Finally, masturbation is clearly a close relative of sex but is generally considered to be distinct from it for the simple reason that only one party is involved.

Are these practices ethical? Are they reasonable things to do? Some, to be sure, are not. Rape is unethical, almost by definition, and quite dangerous to victims, as discussed in a later chapter. People occasionally kill themselves masturbating: Blanchard and Hucker (1991) summarize 117 cases of autoerotic asphyxia in two Canadian provinces within fourteen years. And if media violence can make people more violent (it can, even if the likes of Jack Thompson have caricatured this view: see, for example, Anderson et al., 2010), then presumably violent sexual roleplaying can as well.

That said, I think these potentially problematic practices are the exceptions when it comes to sexual behavior. Most of the excuses people come up with for condemning certain kinds of sex don't hold water. Sex can cause unwanted pregnancies or transmit deadly diseases, but pregnancy is easy to avoid, and the risk of infection can be reduced to a low level. Sex can be disgusting (to only one person or to the vast majority of the human population), but simply because something is disgusting doesn't mean it's destructive or dangerous. Sex can violate religious codes, but religious codes by nature rest on belief in supernatural phenomena and are therefore indefensible from an empirical perspective. Sex can even violate prejudices that may well be innate to humans because of their value for evolutionary fitness, like the taboo against incest, but prejudice alone is no justification. For example, Haidt, Bjorklund, and Murphy (2000) told subjects a short story in which two siblings copulated consensually and with a condom. Less than 11 of the 30 subjects judged this to be acceptable, although 23 subjects together made 38 statements that they were dumbfounded, that is, statements "to the effect that they thought an action was wrong but they could not find the words to explain themselves".

This is not to say that blanket relativism is necessarily correct, either:

> It has often been asserted (by some sexologists, sex educators, and sex therapists) that all sexual behaviours are approximately equal. This assertion springs from the confluence of political prejudices, weak research methods, and unquestioning devotion to the received lore. [Brody, 2006, p. 393]

Even if I wouldn't put it as strongly as Brody, I agree with his point that it is unjustifiable and dangerous to *assume* that every flavor of sex is equal. What we need, if we want to make prescriptive claims about sexual behavior—that is, claims about what people *should* do—is true experiments (clinical trials, of a sort) that randomly assign regimes of sexual behaviors and observe the consequences, for behavior as well as for health.[1] Only experiments with random assignment can provide direct evidence of causation or the lack thereof. By and large, such research does not currently exist. In the meantime, we should suspend our scorn. It is inappropriate to condemn that to which we can't attribute potential harm. Hence the title of this chapter.

[1] Although Brody intends to demonstrate that coitus is superior to masturbation and other kinds of sex, at least for women, his research is insufficient for this goal, since it never randomly assigns subjects to coitus versus other-sex or masturbation conditions.

Sexual abstinence

Our ignorance is a double-edged sword. The dearth of experiments on the consequences of sexual behavior vitiates criticism of sexual indulgence, but it also vitiates criticism of sexual abstinence. So, we can't recommend sex any more than we can condemn it.

Perhaps because of the "political prejudices" of which Brody speaks, researchers have historically been less careful to suspend judgment when discussing abstinence than indulgence. For example, Kinsey, Pomeroy, and Martin (1948), who are famously nonchalant in their reporting of such controversial topics as "animal contacts" (bestiality), characterize another writer's claim that the "idea that sex intercourse is necessary for the health of the young man" is "mistaken" as a "moral evaluation" (p. 26), and they say of repeated attempts to stop masturbating "It is difficult to imagine anything better calculated to do permanent damage to the personality of an individual." (p. 514). In fact, the central argument of Jones's (1997) biography of Kinsey is that Kinsey pretended to be an impartial observer, but in reality sought to liberalize American sexual attitudes. Unfortunately, his extensive research on people's actual sexual behavior says nothing about how better or worse off people would be if they made different sexual choices, which I guess comes to show that the is–ought distinction is a perennial problem for scientists.

The sex drive need not exist

Political prejudice or not, though, anti-abstinence is a logical consequence of an idea with a long history among writers on sexuality and widespread acceptance among the public today: the sex drive. By "sex drive", I mean a motivation to seek sexual gratification that varies in a cyclic, time-dependent fashion like homeostatic motivations such as hunger, thirst, fatigue, and the desire to eliminate. The idea is that sex drive gradually builds up over time until it is reset by sexual activity. (The antithetical, less popular notion is that sexual desire eventually atrophies without gratification.) The word "libido" is often used interchangably with "sex drive", but "libido" is closely associated with Freud's peculiar ideas about sexual motivation providing the motivation for everything, so I avoid using it.

Freud (quoted in Apfelbaum, 1984) entertained a hydraulic notion of sex drive, in which "pressure on the walls of the seminal vesicles" had to be relieved by ejaculation. Kinsey et al. (1948) use the term "sexual outlet" to refer to orgasm frequency presumably because it is sex drive that one needs an outlet for. Closely tied to the idea of sex drive, albeit distinct, is the idea that low frequency of sexual activity is destructive to health or psychological functioning—if this idea were true, sex drive would be useful in the same fashion as hunger. Furthering the analogy with hunger, fear of sex has been called "sexual anorexia" (Carnes, 1998).

Recently, however, the notion of sex drive has been questioned. Bockting (2003) describes masturbation as "not a substitute for those who are sexually deprived, but an activity that stimulates and is stimulated by other sexual behavior". Toates (2009) makes similar claims and proposes that "[sexual] frustration does not reflect a pressure build-up arising from some diffuse regulatory substance[...] Rather[...] frustration would be triggered by (a) the thwarting of forward engagement with sexual incentives and (b) intrusive sexual imagery associated with lack of availability." The overall theme is a change of focus from state to stimulus. Toates's final point also suggests a causal role for people's mental imagery on sexual motivation, which is kind of the reverse of the idea that intrusive sexual imagery is a consequence of sex drive.

What empirical evidence can be brought to bear on the question of whether sex drive exists? Again, there are no relevant experiments. It is known that there exists a refractory period, a short time after orgasm during which sexual arousal is inhibited, at least among men (Levin, 2009). However, the few measurements of refractory periods that have been made, all in young men, have yielded intervals from orgasm to erection or from one orgasm to another on the order of 15 minutes (citing from Levin, 2009: Ekmekçioğlu, Inci, Demirci, & Tatlişen, 2005; Aversa et al., 2000; Mondaini et al., 2003). If the sex drive has more than a slight effect on sexual behavior, it must operate on the same timescale as intervals between instances of sexual activity in real life: hours, days, months, or years. Consider `http://reddit.com/r/NoFap`, an Internet community dedicated to abstinence from masturbation. Its users, who humorously call themselves "fapstronauts", characterize abstinence from masturbation as "the ultimate challenge"; their lapses should therefore be a clear example of the sex drive in action. But fapstronauts measure their time since last masturbatory orgasm in days, not minutes or hours, and consider 90 days a milestone. The refractory period is too short to play a role here.

One prediction of the notion of sex drive is negative relationships between various sources of orgasms. (By a "negative relationship", I mean that the more frequent one source of orgasm, the less frequent another.) In particular, laypeople sometimes suppose that nocturnal emission exists in order to keep the sex drive from growing too intense when one doesn't have enough orgasms while awake, and similarly that masturbation exists to compensate for insufficient sex. Data on the former point is scarce; in fact, data on anything about nocturnal emission is almost nonexistent. Kinsey et al. (1948) weakly suggest a negative relationship but don't examine the question quantitatively. Yu (2012) conducted a survey of 52 men that focused on pornography use and dream content. He found that nocturnal-emission frequency was negatively correlated with masturbation frequency; among several pairs of measures, the strongest relationship was a Spearman correlation of $-.41$.

There is more data on the relationship between masturbation frequency and sex frequency. The overall picture, while not consistent, is generally damaging to the idea of sex drive. Zamboni and Crawford (2002), using a large sample size of 543, found a small *positive* correlation (+.17) between masturbation frequency and sex frequency for both genders. Abramson (1973) found a positive correlation between masturbation frequency and sex frequency among women. Similarly, Davidson (1984) and Pinkerton, Bogart, Cecil, and Abramson (2002) found positive relationships between masturbation frequency and number of sex partners among women. Regnerus, Price, and Gordon (2017), using a large nationally representative sample of Americans, found a weak positive relationship among women and a weak negative relationship among men, both of which varied according to other variables such as whether the subject was married and the subject's reported sexual contentment. On the other hand, there are several failures to find significant correlations (Clifford, 1978; Greenberg, 1972; Kontula & Haavio-Mannila, 2002; and among men only, Abramson, 1973).

I know of a single relevant animal study. Thomsen and Soltis (2004) observed the masturbation patterns of wild male Japanese macaques. Masturbation rates were very high by human standards, with multiple instances per hour being typical. The presented data doesn't directly address the issue, but it suggests a negative relationship between masturbation and sex. On the subject of masturbation rates in general, and animals in particular, I reviewed literature with an eye to comparing typical masturbation rates between species (see appendix: http://arfer.net/w/esa/animast). The range goes from stallions, which seem to typically masturbate 10 times per day, to common chimpanzees, in which masturbation has only ever been observed in unusual rearing conditions. Among the species that have been studied, humans (or at least, American adults) have a fairly intermediate rate.

A recent sex survey with a sample size on the order of Kinsey et al.'s is the National Health and Social Life Survey (Laumann, Gagnon, Michael, & Michaels, 1994). I ran my own analysis of this dataset (for details, see appendix: http://arfer.net/w/esa/sexmastf) and found no correlation between sex frequency and masturbation frequency among women, and a small negative correlation (Kendall $\tau = -.1$) among men.

What can we conclude? We have at most weak support for the notion of sex drive. I suggest we disbelieve in the sex drive until it's more convincingly demonstrated. In fact, a full-blown sex drive is not necessary to explain sexual self-control failures. We could instead attribute such failures to three phenomena that also play roles in drug addiction:

1. A withdrawal phase in which desire does increase over time, but only for a relatively short time after the last indulgence. (Presumably, this effect can be attributed to gross changes in neurotransmitter concentrations in the brain.)
2. Stimulus exposure (i.e., a reminder of sex or drugs).
3. Spontaneous lapses in persistence without any changes in the relevant incentives. (For example, a result of the experiment of Luhmann, Ishida, & Hajcak, 2011, I learned of from personal communication is that, not infrequently, subjects would wait a few seconds for a delayed reward before spontaneously giving up and taking the smaller, immediately available reward.)

The adaptive value of sexuality is an open question

Why have animals evolved to have sex? The obvious answer, "for reproduction", is at odds with the diversity of non-reproductive sexual behavior. Some non-reproductive sexual behavior may exist merely by accident, but there's a variety of ways non-reproductive sexual behavior may otherwise benefit animals. There's no ready answer to the general question of why animals have sex.

Contents

The issue

Why has natural selection allowed sexual affect and sexual behavior to flourish, particularly in humans? The obvious answer is that sexual affect motivates sexual behavior, and sexual behavior is necessary for reproduction. But only a small subset of sexual behavior is actually capable of producing offspring. Why has evolution preserved such things as masturbation, oral sex, homosexuality, and sex after menopause?

I should first of all point out that we can't blame any one weird culture or historical accident, since non-reproductive sexual behavior can be found throughout world history. Pederasty was practiced in medieval Japan (Childs, 1980) as well as in ancient Greece (Percy, 2005), the *Florentine Codex* mentions gay sex among the Aztecs (Kimball, 1993), the *Kama Sutra* discusses fellatio in detail, and in ancient Egyptian mythology, Ra created Shu and Nefnut through masturbation (Armour, 2001). (And on the flipside, if you took the popular claim that masturbation is universal at face value, you might be surprised to learn of peoples in the Central African Republic and the Democratic Republic of the Congo who aren't even aware that masturbation exists; Hewlett & Hewlett, 2010.) Non-reproductive sex isn't even unique to humans: see the Wikipedia article "Non-reproductive sexual behavior in animals" for an impressive laundry list.[1]

[1] Surprisingly, in at least one species, male–male anal sex can be ultimately reproductive. Levan et al. (2009) had virgin male flour beetles copulate anally once, then had each member of these pairs copulate with a female once. 7% of the females produced offspring who were apparently fathered by the male partner of their mate. Apparently, in these cases, a spermatophore was emitted by the partner, stuck to the mate, and impregnated the female during mating.

Unfortunately, the extant research doesn't clearly support any one explanation of all these behaviors across all these species. Perhaps this shouldn't be a surprise. In this chapter, I enumerate some of the available explanations and the evidence for them. They aren't mutually exclusive, but nor are there any proposals of how to integrate them into a coherent theory of non-reproductive sexual behavior. Therefore, the adaptive value of sexuality—the one domain of life that evolutionary psychology would presumably most easily explain—is in fact an open question.

Spandrelism

The most parsimonious explanation is that non-reproductive sexual behavior is a spandrel. That is, natural selection created a motivation to seek genital stimulation because this motivation makes animals more likely to reproduce, and it is merely an accident of evolution that this motivation also gets animals to do useless things like masturbate.

Lloyd (2006), for example, argues that orgasm in women is a

spandrel of orgasm in men, the idea being that female orgasm is of little consequence for fitness but male orgasm is strongly selected for. By contrast, Lloyd doesn't doubt that the clitoris has an adaptive function of encouraging coitus (Smith, 2005), although I would think this a more likely candidate for spandrelism. Consider that the clitoris is a homologue of the penis with no direct reproductive function, just like men's breasts are (usually) nonfunctional equivalents of women's breasts. Consider also that contrary to both (a) the natural a priori expectation that women would only orgasm from something like coitus and (b) the idea that there is no vaginal orgasm, just vaginal stimulation that also happens to stimulate part of the clitoris (Kinsey, Pomeroy, Martin, & Gebhard, 1953, p. 582; Koedt, 1970), women are capable of distinct clitoral and vaginal orgasms: clitoral stimulation alone can produce orgasm in most women, and Komisaruk, Gerdes, and Whipple (1997) showed that orgasm can be induced from vaginal stimulation in women with complete spinal cord injury, whose clitorises must therefore be numb. *Vaginal* orgasm has obvious utility for fitness; with that taken for granted, the clitoris and its orgasm are the seeming oddballs. Things only get odder, though, given (what I believe to be) the common belief by sex therapists that clitoral orgasm is easier to achieve than vaginal orgasm. This idea has some support in the observation of Kinsey et al. (1953) that women orgasm from 95% of masturbation events (p. 132) but only 70–77% of coitus events (p. 393). If masturbation is more reliably reinforced than reproductive sex, a spandrel argument becomes more difficult to believe.

One of the weirdest examples of non-reproductive sex is mounting among desert-grasslands whiptail lizards, *Aspidoscelis uniparens*.[2] *A. uniparens* is all-female and reproduces exclusively by parthenogenesis, that is, development from unfertilized egg cells. However, during part of the ovarian cycle (after ovulation), individuals will mount other individuals, like the males of the sexually reproducing ancestor species *Aspidoscelis inornata*,[3] and during follicular development, *A. uniparens* individuals are receptive to mounting, just like *A. inornata* females (Woolley, Sakata, & Crews, 2004). This "pseudosexual" behavior is consequential insofar as mounting seems to increase the number of eggs laid by the receptive animal (Crews, Grassman, & Lindzey, 1986). Crews et al. reason that this dependency is a consequence of *A. uniparens*'s unusual history, which includes hybridization. I imagine that it will disappear from the species eventually, so long as *A. uniparens* never regains males.

² Formerly *Cnemidophorus uniparens*.
³ Formerly *Cnemidophorus inornatus*.

There are some species in which certain sexual behaviors have been observed at least once but only rarely. For example, Starin (2004) observed just five instances of masturbation by males in a five-and-a-half–year field study of western red colobus, a type of monkey. Behavior so rare and with no obvious consequences presumably has no function, and is under little selective pressure to disappear.

Social functions

(No, not that kind of social function.)

Bonobos, one of the two species of chimpanzee, are famous for their sociosexuality (Manson, Perry, & Parish, 1997), particularly tribadism (usually called "genitogenital rubbing" in writing about bonobos). Observation of the circumstances in which tribadism most frequently occurs has suggested that tribadism can be a means of reconciliation after conflict (Hohmann & Fruth, 2000), integration of new females into a group (Idani, 1991, who also points out that males frequently copulate with immigrant females and suggests that coitus thus serves a similarly relationship-solidifying function), or regulation of social tension that arises during eating (Hohmann & Fruth, 2000; Kano, 1980). Li, Yin, and Zhou (2007) observed Tibetan macaques, which can only conceive during their mating season, copulating many times outside of the mating season. As Hohmann and Fruth say of bonobos, Li et al. suggests that this non-reproductive sexual behavior could have a function of reducing conflict ("approximately 20% of the matings during the birth season took place in aggressive situations, which is a higher percentage than in the mating season"). Li et al. also suggests that females copulate outside the mating season in exchange for resources such as food or "favorable places".⁴

⁴ A more widely known example of "prostitution" in animals is Hunter and Davis's (1998) observation of mated female Adélie penguins copulating with males other than their mate in exchange for rocks on which to lay their eggs. But in this case, the harlotry could conceive, so it isn't a clear example of non-repro-

ductive sex.

Intuitively, I think the idea that sexuality has been co-opted by evolution to serve social in addition to reproductive functions makes sense. Since reproduction was already an important reason for conspecifics to interact with each other, it would've been a natural choice for a parsimonious designer to extend into a general mechanism for navigating and shaping the social world. This idea also provides a possible explanation for why human sexual behavior is so frequently and thickly intertwined with social relationships, despite the appeal of spontaneous anonymous sex.

I feel obliged to point out that these ideas don't imply that sex is a good way for modern humans to communicate. As Apfelbaum (1984) argues convincingly, sex isn't even an effective form of communication about simple sexual matters.

Disposal of suboptimal sperm

A man who's trying to impregnate a woman needs to strike a balance as to the number of sperm he ejaculates. For, a high concentration of sperm in a woman's reproductive tract increases the chance of successful conception only up to a point. This is best demonstrated by the findings that (1) in vitro, as the sperm-to-egg ratio increases past some point, the chance of conception decreases (e.g., Tsunoda & Chang, 1975) and (2) men with polyzoospermia, who emit very high numbers of sperm per ejaculate, are less fertile although in-vitro fertilization with their sperm is unimpaired (Tournaye et al., 1997). Baker and Bellis (1993) offer two possible explanations: enzymes released by large numbers of sperm can destroy an egg, and fertilization of a single egg by multiple sperm yields a non-viable zygote. At any rate, this need for balance explains Baker and Bellis's observation that men emit more sperm per copulation the longer the intervals between copulations, effectively "topping up" the woman to an optimum level.

An additional complication to this balancing act, Baker and Bellis postulate, is that sperm grow less effective as they age. If sperm are emitted in first-in-first-out order, this raises the danger of a man who's only emitting a limited number of sperm failing to emit the best sperm available. Non-reproductive ejaculation, especially masturbation and nocturnal emission, provide a solution by disposing of sperm in large quantities. Levan, Fedina, and Lewis (2009) concluded that male–male anal copulation among flour beetles serves a similar function.

Practice

When non-reproductive sex is more accessible than reproductive sex, animals might pursue it for practice. Li et al. (2007) noticed that during the mating season, some male macaques wouldn't tolerate other males copulating with females, particularly if the copulating male was adolescent or ranked below the other male. The lower stakes outside of the mating season would probably be a better time for males to practice sex.

Prophylaxis

Male Cape ground squirrels masturbate to ejaculation frequently, on the order of once a day, sometimes several times a day. Waterman (2010) observed instances of masturbation in a wild population to test several different hypotheses as to its function. She found that (1) the males masturbated more frequently on days during which a female was in estrous, (2) masturbation increased with number of partners, and (3) masturbation was more common after than before or between coitus events. She concluded that the best supported hypothesis is that masturbation is a means of flushing the penis of sexually transmitted pathogens.

One might wonder why Cape ground squirrels don't just urinate to accomplish this function. People are sometimes advised to urinate after sex for this reason (Donovan, 2000). "As a desert-adapted species, however," Waterman writes, "Cape ground squirrels produce very concentrated urine and rarely urinate". The squirrels minimize waste of moisture through masturbation by swallowing their ejaculate (apparently, they find autofellatio much less difficult than humans do).

Tan et al. (2009) observed female greater short-nosed fruit bats (*Cynopterus sphinx*) licking the shaft and base of their mate's penis during coitus. (So unlike the other non-reproductive sexual behaviors discussed in this chapter, this behavior occurs only in an apparently reproductive context.) Tan et al. make a similar suggestion: saliva may kill pathogens and thus reduce the spread of disease.

Prolonging coitus

Tan et al. noticed that the longer the coitus event, the more time the female spent licking. This might be just because a longer coitus event means the females have more time to do this, but it could also be that the licking prolongs the coitus, which in turn might have benefits such as increasing the chance of conception.[5]

[5] Yet another hypothesis Tan et al. suggest is that the licking helps with mate choice by helping the female identify a feature of the male's genotype. But by the time coitus is occurring, it's too late for the female to exercise mate choice—unless greater short-nosed fruit bats can abort pregnancies in response to environmental cues, as in the Bruce effect (Bruce, 1959). At least some bats can abort or reabsorb an embryo if food is scarce (Grindal, Collard, Brigham, & Barclay, 1992).

Discouraging reproduction

The award for originality goes to Cox (1995). Cox draws an analogy between the human foreskin and hymen. Each serves as a barrier, however slight, to coitus: the foreskin needs to be retracted and the hymen needs to be burst. (Cox also points out several parallels in how cultures regard the foreskin and the hymen.) But the foreskin also *facilitates* masturbation. Cox reasons that the purpose of the foreskin and hymen is to discourage early reproduction, the idea being that humans are best off establishing themselves socially and economically before investing resources in raising children. Masturbation, at least in men, exists as a substitute for coitus and therefore a disincentive. (But see the previous chapter for surveys that are unsupportive of this last assertion.)

Diversity of sexual preferences is to be expected

We tend to classify people's sexual preferences into sexual orientations, such as "straight", "gay", and "bisexual". I argue that, on the contrary, we should expect sexual preferences to be just as idiosyncratic as ice-cream preferences. Indeed, there are many ways in which familiar sexual orientations do not seem to adequately describe people's sexual preferences and sexual behavior. While it is legitimate to want to categorize sexual preferences, laypeople and scientists alike have been too eager to do so with scant regard for empirical reality. A misleading taxonomy is worse than no taxonomy at all.

Contents

Introduction

In the contemporary West, it is taken for granted that sexual preferences—that is, what things people find sexually appealing—fall into a few discrete categories, which are called sexual orientations. Invariably, heterosexuality and homosexuality are considered sexual orientations (although some consider the word "homosexuality" stigmatizing for historical reasons). Usually, bisexuality is included. Many other extensions to this taxonomy exist, although none are popular among laymen. Among these extensions are a four-orientation model in which asexuality is included as a fourth orientation; the Kinsey scale, in which there is "Exclusively heterosexual with no homosexual", "Exclusively homosexual", and five intermediate points (Kinsey, Pomeroy, & Martin, 1948, p. 638); an added distinction between "tops" and "bottoms" (insertive or dominating versus receptive or submissive); a dual-axis model in which preferences for age are distinct from preferences for gender (Seto, 2012); and the Klein grid, which comprises 27 seven-point items (on gay–straight axes) organized into seven features and three time-points (Weinrich et al., 1993).

So, how well are real people's real sexual preferences described by these taxonomies? In everyday life, we rarely ask this question—we assume that the gay–straight dichotomy or gay–bi–straight trichotomy is correct and thence do all our reasoning about people's sexual preferences. Should these models be wrong, it is easy to see how great harm could arise from slavish application of them, from trying to pound square pegs into round holes. I need not provide any anecdotes about the misery people undergo when they feel unsure about their sexual orientation: popular media and likely the reader's own life are full of such anecdotes. How much more inescapable this suffering would be if the root problem were not mere ambiguity about which sexual orientation one belonged to, but the nonexistence of a sexual orientation that fits! The situation could then only be resolved with stoic apathy, denial of one's own feelings, or the invention of yet another sexual orientation. (As if we needed another letter added onto "LGBTQAOMGWTF-BBQ".)

I'm tempted to claim that sexual orientation, considered as a psychological theory, is wrong. But I can't, because, as I was saying earlier, sexual orientation isn't any one theory or model; it's more like a big family of models with the lay dichotomy as common ancestor. The family as a whole can't be falsified. Faced with falsificatory evidence for any one model, one could extend the model into a new one that can handle the new evidence. Falsification is yet more difficult because sexual orientation, although often employed in an explanatory fashion (particularly by laymen), is more descriptive than explanatory: it says a lot more about the exact phenomena of interest (sexual attraction and behavior) than about any supposed causes. A careful thinker wouldn't claim that Joe has sex with Bob *because* Joe is gay; they would instead attribute the causal power to whatever they think causes male–male sexual attraction and behavior to begin with, and say that the attraction that led Joe to have sex with Bob is part of what *constitutes* Joe's homosexuality. There are then few causal chains within these models to test, and the only way they're accountable to empirical reality is that they have to include everybody, or at least, every sexual-preference pattern that can be found in more than a dozen people. The only other constraint on these models is that they have to be models, in the sense that they need to make only finitely many distinctions and they need to have halfway-coherent theories behind them.

There exists a more sophisticated philosophy for scientific models, which is to assume that all models are, in the final analysis, false, and change the focus from finding a correct model to finding the most useful model (see Arfer & Luhmann, 2015, for a related discussion). How exactly usefulness should be measured is, of course, context-dependent. It then becomes difficult to talk about how good a model is in abstract terms. A model that's excellent for one purpose could be poor for another. I think, however, that the onus is very much on the proponents of sexual orientation to demonstrate it is useful for anything other than breeding confusion and hatred among ordinary people.

At any rate, I can't falsify sexual orientation. The most I can do here is to enumerate some potential problems for any sexual-orientation taxonomy. These gotchas will mostly be ways sexual preferences can be diverse, which may remind you of the lists of non-reproductive sexual practices in the previous chapter. (But I'll give much less attention to animals than last time, because, for reasons that aren't clear to me but might just be differences of discipline (e.g., ethology versus sociology), scientists are much less hasty to classify the sexual preferences of animals than of humans.) Some are more specifically problematic to one model than another. Taken together, though, they're strong reason not to put too much faith in the idea of sexual orientation.

Non-sexual preferences obviously tend to be diverse

Instead of sex, let's think about ice cream for a moment.[1] As a rule, people like ice cream. But they don't all like ice cream in exactly the same way. Consider yourself. Maybe you like vanilla. Maybe you like chocolate. Maybe you like both. Maybe you like vanilla a lot but chocolate only a little. Maybe you like chocolate in ice-cream sodas but when you're getting a cone it's vanilla with rainbow sprinkles or nothing. Maybe you enjoy the idea of vanilla but chocolate always seems to taste better in practice. Maybe you have pleasant associations with chocolate because it reminds you of your happiest childhood days, but vanilla appeals to you in a more direct, less sentimental way. Maybe you have much stronger opinions about soft-serve versus hard ice cream than flavor, so flavor, by contrast, is immaterial. Maybe you like strawberry. Maybe you like Pan-Galactic Gargle Chip (not that you have any idea what it tastes like, since it doesn't exist, but it sounds delicious for some reason). Maybe ice cream in general fails to excite you. Maybe you're just not a fan of ice cream, however good it tastes, and at times you wish that man had never domesticated the cow.

[1] The title-text of North (2011) reads "did you know that in real life all those stats for how often the average person thinks about sex are ACTUALLY about ice cream?"

While we can classify people's ice-cream preferences in all sorts of ways, it would clearly be absurd to take such a taxonomy too seriously. People's preferences, examined in sufficient detail, are bound to be eccentric and varied, as is to be expected considering the wide variety of things that could somehow affect their preferences. There's no accounting for taste. (While we psychologists assume that there must be *some* causal chain behind a person's preferences, it can be arbitrarily obscure in any individual case.)

Simply put, why should we expect sexual preferences to be

fundamentally different from ice-cream preferences? Correlations with respect to gender don't make idiosyncrasy disappear.

To make this ice-cream analogy more concrete, consider two simple stimulus-norming studies I conducted on Amazon Mechanical Turk in May and June of 2012 (Arfer, 2012). In each, subjects were shown 12 images and were asked to pick the image they found most appealing, the image they found second-most appealing, and the image they found third-most appealing. The primary difference between the two studies was that the first used photographs of desserts and the second used photographs of women, most of them semi-nude and in sexually provocative poses. Another relevant difference was that the second study was open only to Americans, whereas the first had no restrictions on country, so it probably included a lot of Indians, for example (Ipeirotis, 2010).

- The dessert study had 94 subjects. All but one of the images were selected at least once as a first choice, and all the images were selected at least twice as a second choice and as a third choice. There were 84 unique first–second–third selections in the sample, or 66 disregarding order.
- The sex study had 155 subjects (some of whom had also participated in the dessert study). Considering only subjects who stated they were male and sexually attracted to women (who should, of course, have had less diverse preferences than the whole sample), there were 88 subjects. Among these subjects, every image was selected at least twice for each of the three choices, and there were 86 unique first–second–third selections, or 70 disregarding order.

These findings don't exactly prove my point, considering issues such as how subjects had no way to indicate indifference and the lack of random assignment to studies, but I consider them supportive. Certainly, the second study flies in the face of the stereotype that men have homogeneous and predictable sexual preferences.

Preferences are fickle

One additional lesson can be drawn from the ice-cream analogy described above. Even though ice-cream preferences can be affected by many things, from one's genes to other people's opinions, we know of no reliable way to change our preferences deliberately.

We can't freely choose our preferences. On the contrary, preferences are, by definition, one of the fundamental causes of our choices. The moral is that despite popular belief, even if genes had no influence on sexual preferences, it wouldn't follow that sexual preferences are freely chosen, nor that sexual preferences are otherwise easy to change when one wants to. From this perspective, the APA task force's (Glassgold et al., 2009) conclusion that no existing gay-to-straight conversion therapy is effective, and Quinsey's (2008) conclusion that treatment can't change the true preferences of sex offenders, aren't surprising. And the claim that "sexual orientation" is a better term than "sexual preference" because "preference" "suggests a degree of voluntary choice" (Committee on Lesbian and Gay Concerns, American Psychological Association, 1991, p. 973) is nonsensical.

Just how fickle preferences can be is perhaps best demonstrated by Ariely, Loewenstein, and Prelec (2006). In a series of three experiments on college students, some subjects were asked whether they would pay money to attend a poetry recital by their instructor and others were asked if they would attend the recital for a fee paid to them. This manipulation affected how people evaluated the poetry recital. In Experiment 1, for example, 35% of subjects initially asked to pay said they would attend the poetry recital if it were free, compared to only 8% of subjects initially offered money to attend it. Experiment 3 showed that, amazingly, similar changes in valuation persisted even if subjects heard a sample of the poetry recital first (so they had a concrete sense of what it would be like) and were shown the two experimental conditions and how they were assigned. We are obliged to believe that subjects did not have a firm preference about whether attending the poetry recital was a desirable or undesirable experience. They were so uncertain about their own likes and dislikes on the matter that they stuck to whatever cue had been handed to them, even when they knew that the cue was completely uninformative. I submit that if people can be so uncertain and confused about their preferences for an experience as simple as a poetry recital, they are likely to be all the more confused about their preferences for romantic partners and sexual experiences.

Identity vs. attraction vs. behavior

Often, sexual orientations aren't considered exactly classes of sexual preferences. They may construed as classes of sexual behavior, whereby one's sexual orientation describes who one has sex with rather than who one finds attractive. Or they may be construed as identities, whereby one's sexual orientation is whatever group one *says* one belongs to. Or they may be construed as some combination of all three. While it makes sense that epidemiologists should group people according to who they've had sex with, and sociologists should group people according to who they identify with, it can be dangerous to conflate the three characteristics. Such conflation happens, for example, every time a researcher tries to measure sexual preferences by asking subjects what they identify as, which is the most common way of measuring sexual preferences (oops).

Dissociation of attraction and behavior

Sexual feelings are one motivation among many, so people don't always act according to their sexual feelings. Obviously, most people experience sexual feelings for years before they have sex for the first time: sexual attraction typically appears at age 10 (McClintock & Herdt, 1996), whereas 17 is a typical age of sexual debut in the US (Cavazos-Rehg et al., 2009). Conversely, it isn't uncommon for men who have feelings for other men but not for women to marry women anyway (Butler, 2006), perhaps only to divorce years later when they conclude they'll never change and they've only been living a lie.

Dissociation of identity and attraction or identity and behavior

Not merely some but *most* people who are attracted to or have sex with the same sex don't identify as gay (Savin-Williams, 2006, citing Laumann, Gagnon, Michael, & Michaels, 1994). Hence the awkward term "men who have sex with men", commonly abbreviated "MSM", which is widely used in research.

"Situational homosexuality", that is, sex among people in a

single-gender setting who would apparently otherwise be having heterosexual sex, is another kind of disjunction between identity and behavior. Gagnon and Simon (1968) give 30% as a low estimate for the proportion of prisoners who have sex with other (same-gender) inmates, which is clearly higher than the proportions of gay identity or same-gender sex in the general population. Evans-Pritchard (1970) describes an institutionalized form of situational homosexuality among the precolonial Azande, a Central African people. Bachelors in certain military companies would officially marry younger males, who "might have been anywhere between about twelve and twenty years of age" (p. 1,430). The "boy-wife" not only had sex with his husband but also performed grunt work such as carrying his husband's shield, drawing water, and cooking.

Instability over time

Mock and Eibach (2012) examined change in stated sexual orientation over a ten-year period in a large probability sample of adults, the National Survey of Midlife Development in the United States. The options were "heterosexual", "homosexual", and "bisexual". The vast majority of subjects chose "heterosexual" both times, but 18 of 1,342 women and 9 of 1,152 men who were straight in Wave 1 switched to gay or bi in Wave 2. Gay men were also reasonably but not perfectly stable: of the 21 in Wave 1, 1 switched to straight and 1 switched to bi. But Wave 1's lesbians (11) and bisexuals (17 female and 17 male) were overall no more likely to stay their initial orientation than switch to one of the other two. Similar results was obtained by Ott, Corliss, Wypij, Rosario, and Austin (2011), who used 5,887 males and 7,953 females from the four-wave Growing Up Today Study and an orientation item with options "completely heterosexual", "mostly heterosexual", "bisexual", "mostly homosexual", "completely homosexual", and "unsure". Over two-year periods starting during adulthood, complete heterosexuals were highly unlikely to change (no more than 7%), gay men were slightly more likely to change (11%), lesbians were somewhat more (35%), and other orientations were at most a little more likely to stay the same than change. Finally, similar results were also obtained by Savin-Williams, Joyner, and Rieger (2012), who used 5,527 men and 6,556 women from waves 3 and 4 of the

National Longitudinal Survey of Adolescent Health, and similar orientation categories as Ott et al. (2011). Over a six-year period, stability was observed in 97% of completely heterosexual men, 88% of completely heterosexual women, 71% of completely homosexual men, 67% of completely homosexual women, and no more than 53% in every other category.

So, while rates of change differ by gender and starting sexual orientation, and change is rare overall, it happens nontrivially: orientation isn't fixed. Change seems particularly common among people who aren't heterosexual to begin with. I would expect people are more willing to change their mind about their orientation if they've already made the mental leap of identifying as something other than the default.

Since all studies I know of on change in sexual orientation over time have relied on self-report, it's hard to say what's actually changing. When a man stops calling himself straight and starts calling himself gay, has he merely changed how he interprets his own feelings, as laypeople assume, or is it actually his sexual preferences that have changed? And what if not only can preferences affect identity but identity can affect preferences? How does honest-to-God sexual behavior fit in here?

Cultural differences

In ancient Greece, pederasty was a social institution. Although there was controversy among contemporaries as to whether pederasty aided in the development of the boy's character or was merely a means of sexual gratification for the adult, just as modern scholars debate its role in ancient society, it was widely acknowledged and not generally stigmatized (Percy, 2005). Since the adult was typically married to a woman at the same time (Stearns, 2009), and the boy presumably married a woman himself in adulthood, neither partner confined their sexual activity to males. Nor are such specialized arrangements consonant with the idea of gender-blind bisexuality.

Sexual preferences for weird stuff

One aspect of sexual preferences that lines up poorly with the idea of sexual orientation is preferences targeted to specific acts, objects, or personal characteristics.[2] de Silva (1999) mentions sexual fantasies, feelings, and behaviors concerning garments, cross-dressing, urine, feces, prepubescent children, animals, dead bodies, and pain and humiliation.[3] Scorolli, Ghirlanda, Enquist, Zattoni, and Jannini (2007), in a survey of Yahoo! Groups (online message boards and mailing lists), concluded that body parts (such as feet) are particularly popular. Scorolli et al. also mention Yahoo! Groups devoted to things as oddly specific as "smoking girls playing with balloons", but at this point it becomes difficult to distinguish parody from reality, as Poe's law would suggest.

[2] Such preferences can be called "fetishes", but that term is also used by clinicians for the narrower case of people whose sexual arousal is *dependent* on something odd rather than merely *facilitated* by it.

[3] You might wonder why things usually associated with unpleasant emotions, like pain, disgust, fear, and shame, would appear as fetishes. Nobody's appetite is whetted by disgusting food; why would anybody's sexual appetite be whetted by disgusting sex? If you will permit me to speculate wildly, I have two suggestions:

- Misattribution of arousal, along the lines of Dutton and Aron (1974), could cause arousal induced by negative affect to be transmuted into sexual arousal.
- Sexuality itself is associated with negative affect, as I discuss in the next chapter. Negative affect could then bring about sexual arousal by means of classical conditioning.

Tying in with the previous theme of instability, Hoffmann (2012) mentions several reports of successful conditioning of sexual appeal in animals and humans, although she adds that in humans, the conditioning is "often weak and short-lived" (p. 67) and seems to depend on several individual differences.

Hyposexuality

Not everybody experiences enough sexual feelings or behavior to satisfy popular notions of straight or gay.

Children

One important example is young children. I earlier stated that sexual attraction begins around age 10, but masturbation and a few other arguably sexual behaviors, such as examining other children's genitals, are not unheard of in children half that age (Larsson, 2000). In Okami, Olmstead, and Abramson (1997), 77% of interviewed mothers "reported that their child had engaged in sex play prior to age six" (p. 343). Furthermore, sexual behavior in young children does not seem to be related to sexual abuse by adults (Drach, Wientzen, & Ricci, 2001), suggesting it is not merely recapitulation of abuse. At the same time, Okami et al. (1997) indicate that attempts at coitus, and Larsson (2000) indicates that attempts at any penetration (vaginal, anal, or oral), are rare in this age group. I'd thus say it's quite ambiguous how prepubescent sexuality relates to the more familiar forms of sexuality in adolescents and adults.

Asexuality and related orientations

Thanks to a website called the Asexual Visibility and Education Network (AVEN; http://www.asexuality.org), there is also an increasing number of people who describe themselves as asexual. "Asexual" refers to people who are of an age at which sexual attraction is normal but who claim not to experience it at all (Chasin, 2011; Yule, Brotto, & Gorzalka, 2015), despite normal endocrine function (e.g., not being castrated) and not taking potential anaphrodisiacs (e.g., SSRIs). Some asexuals have feelings they describe as sexual desire, while others do not. Some asexuals enjoy masturbation, while others see no appeal in it. Some asexuals are repulsed by sex, while others are indifferent or even interested despite their lack of the usual motive. The large AVEN community also includes people who claim a variety of other novel orientations (Walton, Lykins, & Bhullar, 2016), such as demisexuality (sexual attraction only to people with whom the subject has a pre-existing emotional connection), gray-A (somewhere between total asexuality and more conventional sexual feelings), and romantic orientations distinct from sexual orientations (such that one could be a homoromantic heterosexual, or an aromantic bisexual, or a biromantic asexual).

It isn't wholly unreasonable to think that people who claim these exotic orientations are just being special snowflakes—that is, that much of this diversity is either nonexistent or exists only because people believe they experience it. But before we have data other than self-report to help settle the issue, I'm inclined to grant asexuals, demisexuals, and so on the benefit of the doubt. I think there's real diversity in sexual preferences within this population that's unaddressed by the lay trichotomy. Is this not very much the sort of thing that the ice-cream analogy suggests should exist?[4] Although, as always, I don't think inventing more orientations is the best response to the issue.

[4] It's backwards for me to say this, because—full disclosure—I first came up with the central idea of this chapter when I was reading about all of AVEN's idiosyncratic orientations. I thought "Geez! How do you know when to stop making more of 'em?" Then I realized that this issue, along with many others, wouldn't exist if we weren't committed to making discrete taxonomies of sexual preferences in the first place. It was at that point that I thought of the ice-cream analogy. I see AVEN's proliferation of sexual orientations as an argumentum ad absurdum against the concept of sexual orientation.

Masturbation

Note that most identified-heterosexual men masturbate (Herbenick et al., 2010) although there's nothing heterosexual about masturbation. (Yes, one can have heterosexual fantasies while masturbating, but one can have heterosexual fantasies while doing anything.) The incidence of masturbation in children under 6 and asexuals also suggests that masturbation is caused by sexual preferences that are distinct from the sort of sexual preferences we usually think about.

So, in conclusion, do you advocate blanket relativism with respect to sexual preferences?

By no means. Truth be told, when I was doing the research for this chapter, I was sometimes surprised to find more consistency in sexual preferences for gender than I'd expected. I thought, for example, that I'd readily find (perhaps in Francoeur & Noonan, 2004) examples of sexual identities accepted as normal by non-Western cultures that didn't involve gender-bending (as two-spiritism does) but clearly didn't line up with hetero-, homo-, or bisexuality. Instead, the above section "Cultural differences" has only the one example of Greek pederasty. It seems that non-Western cultures tend only to have heterosexuality (perhaps with a bit of not-very-systematic homosexuality on the side), situational homosexuality, and (more rarely) fairly exclusive homosexuality or fairly even bisexuality. Also, I found three papers showing surprisingly good concordance between sexual identity and lower-level phenomena, at least in men. Snowden, Wichter, and Gray (2008) found that gender preference implied by performance in priming tasks is strongly predictive of identity. Jiang et al. (2006) found that identity predicted whether subliminal perception of a nude picture of a man or a woman would attract attention to its location. Finally, Ponseti et al. (2009) were able to predict individual identity with fMRI using group differences in BOLD response between 12 straight men and 14 gay men.

What moral, then, we can draw from all this? I suggest the following:

- Sexual orientation is not a natural kind, that is, a fundamental natural taxonomy.
- Don't confuse descriptions of sexual preferences with their causes.
- Don't assume that gender is the only important aspect of sexual preferences.
- Don't assume that sexual preferences are stable over time, but don't expect to be able to change them at will, either.
- Don't forget that preferences, behavior, and identity are distinct. In both everyday life and in research, examine

what you're actually interested in. As Savin-Williams (2006) says (p. 43), "To assess STDs or HIV transmission, measure sexual behavior. To assess interpersonal attachments, measure sexual/romantic attraction. To assess political ideology, measure sexual identity."

- Decide whether to construe unusual sexual preferences as pathological by considering their consequences, not the degree to which they're unusual. (But now I'm practically repeating myself from the earlier chapter about practices.) Relatedly, if somebody's upset about their sexual preferences (whether they're a man disgusted at his desire for other men or a woman frustrated by her lack of desire), consider that either the preferences themselves or the subject's attitudes and reactions towards those preferences, or even some combination of both, could be fruitfully construed as the root problem. There is no magical dividing line between sexual preferences that are good and natural and that you just have to learn to tolerate and sexual preferences that are horrible and vile and that you must figure out how to change.

In summary, don't be essentialist about sexual preferences.

If we absolutely must construct taxonomies of sexual preferences, the case of discrete emotions might be a good model of how to proceed. Despite our many intuitions about what emotions exist, what causes them, what they do, and so on, researchers haven't hesitated to dream up new models of discrete emotion that bear little resemblance to lay concepts. There are even people who think about discrete emotions roughly the way I think about sexual orientations. For example, Barrett (2012) argues that emotions exist partly as "social reality", the same way that I would say that "gay" as a kind of person, an identity, exists only as a social construct even though it has a basis in trends in sexual preferences that exist independently of anybody's beliefs. Arguably, the field of emotion has too many competing theories, but this is surely better than everybody being unreasonably committed to a particular culture's lay theory.

An ongoing study by me and a collaborator (http://arfer.net/projects/galaxy) demonstrates another strategy. We are giving subjects a long list of types of sex partners, sexual activities, and sexual themes and asking how attractive they find each. We will then investigate statistically how these many individual preferences are organized. By avoiding a priori commitment to any particular taxonomy of sexual preference, we will hopefully maximize our chances of detecting whatever trends really exist.

Humans are ambivalent about sex because they fear death

Why do strange, apparently useless sexual taboos appear in all human societies? Experiments show that people associate sexuality with animals and the body, and thus with mortality. It appears that social norms ranging from disapproval of prostitution to the ideal of romantic love exist, in part, to provide us a kind of symbolic immortality and buffer us from existential threat. There exist other potential explanations for sexual taboos, but the overall picture is not favorable to anyone who would seek to free human sexuality from artificial restrictions.

Contents

Erotophobia and ambivalence

The many exotic and bizarre manifestations of human sexuality; the cultural and religious taboos; the vows of celibacy; the often psychologically based sexual dysfunctions; the segregation of the sexes in

> many cultures; the veiling of women's faces and the
> binding of their feet; the secrecy, guilt, shame, and
> anxiety surrounding sexuality; and the romanticiza-
> tion of sexual relations in literature and real life
> throughout the ages all attest to the unique complexi-
> ties of human sexuality. [Goldenberg, Pyszczynski,
> McCoy, Greenberg, & Solomon, 1999, p. 1,175]

As I discussed in the preface, people have all sorts of attitudes and
societies have all sorts of rules about sexuality. Perhaps you've noticed how strange these can be.

It makes evolutionary sense that people should be disgusted
by potentially dangerous activities like incest and bestiality. (The
danger of incest being the investment of one's parental resources
into low-fitness, inbred children, and the danger of bestiality being
zoonosis and even injury, as in the famous Enumclaw horse-sex
case; Sullivan, 2005). Accordingly, Fessler and Navarrete (2003)
(p. 407) cite findings of such disgust in the West, the Pacific Is-
lands, and Sub-Saharan Africa.

But why should we be frightened or disgusted by, say, masturbation or tribadism, especially if such activities do in fact have
adaptive value (as was ambivalently suggested in a previous chapter), and animals, although they don't universally participate in
such activities, never express aversion to them like ours? And this
issue is but one part of the vast and mysterious web of rules about
sexuality and (more generally) the flesh that permeate human society. Such rules are often associated with religion: Christianity,
thanks to Gnosticism, tends to associate sexual purity and incorpo-
reality with godliness, both Jewish and Islamic texts prescribe
death penalties for things as innocuous as gay sex and premarital
coitus, and the *Kama Sutra* has all kinds of odd rules for enjoying
the many sexual acts it describes (Goldenberg et al., 1999). Begin-
ning under Victorianism, secular intellectuals like physicians got
into the act with pseudomedical excuses (Stearns, 2009), as by
blaming masturbation for insanity. And some of the most general
bodily rules are attributed to vague needs for privacy or decency:
in the West and in many other societies, bathrooms are sex-segre-
gated, farting is embarrassing, sexual and scatological references
must be minimized and euphemized in polite conversation—and
however acceptable nudity is in special circumstances like medical
examinations, beaches, saunas, nudist colonies, athletics, and the-

ater, it's out of the question in everyday social interaction, no matter how little the practical reasons for wearing clothing (protection from cold, sun, bugs, etc.) apply in the local environment. Finally, in the West, notice that sexuality is considered to be among the things that children need to be protected from (Arfer, 2011). Here's a great example of how nonsensical sexual taboos can appear from an outsider's perspective: Goldenberg et al. (1999), citing Powdermaker (1933), say (p. 1,174) "the Lesu of the South Pacific accept female masturbation any time a woman becomes aroused as long as she does it by pressing the heel of the right foot against her genitals; the use of one's hands for masturbation is strictly forbidden."

The most important point to be made here is that taboos and regulations about sex and the body *that have no obvious function* are often wildly heterogeneous between cultures but their existence is universal. There isn't a single culture without such taboos. Let me strengthen that claim a bit: there isn't a single culture without sexual taboos. The societies that are sometimes held up as examples of societies without sexual taboos, aren't. For example, Ray (2009) claims "Sweden's full of those people" who don't feel guilty about premarital sex, but most Swedes disapprove of 15-year-old girls having casual sex (Trost & Bergstrom-Walan, 2004). And Ray says "Tahiti is full of those teenagers who have sex before they're married and nobody feels guilt about it", but Tahitians zealously guard the premarital virginity of one kind of teenager: "firstborn daughters in lineages of firstborns" (Bolin, 2004). Not to mention the controversy over Margaret Mead's claims about sexuality in Samoa.

Anyway, the point is, although human societies vary widely in terms of sexual libertarianism, history recalls not a single human society that managed to be as uniformly sex-positive as bonobos. Civilization invariably contains, in a word, erotophobia. In science, the word "erotophobia" usually refers to a dimension of personality that describes the tendency to approach or avoid sexual things (Fisher, White, Byrne, & Kelley, 1988). I'm abusing the word here to refer to much larger-scale, social phenomena. While I expect that there's a meaningful relationship between these two kinds of erotophobia, personal and societal, my concern is mostly with the latter. The fact that everyone wears clothes strikes me as more in need of explanation than the fact that some people are blatantly anxious about sex.

With both erotophobia and appreciation of sexual pleasure being universal features of human societies, it's fair to say that humans, as a species, are ambivalent about sex. "Ambivalence" meaning not mere uncertainty but the coexistence of simultaneous contradictory feelings. As Davis and Whitten (1987) put it, "It is not ethnocentric to conclude that a degree of ambivalnce typifies much sexual behavior" (p. 78). A corollary is that sex-positive feminists who hope to defeat erotophobia and create a sex-positive society are taking on a much greater challenge than they may've anticipated. They're not just fighting Victorianism or Western civilization or religion. They're fighting human nature.

Terror-management theory

Speaking of human nature, let me now expound on what I see as the best available explanation for people's ambivalence about sex and the body. For the first time in this book, there's a wealth of relevant experimental evidence, so I'll be able to make some strong claims.

Theory and findings

Terror-management theory (TMT) postulates that denying personal mortality is a primary human motive (Greenberg, Solomon, & Arndt, 2008). Humans, uniquely among all animals, are intelligent enough to have a sense of self and also to understand that they as agents are certain to eventually stop existing. Thus they create and endorse ideals, philosophies, and social structures that imbue life with symbolic meaning, providing a kind of symbolic immortality. This broad idea is originally due to Ernest Becker, an anthropologist who was inspired by Otto Rank and hence by Freud, but it was first examined experimentally by Jeff Greenberg, Tom Pyszczynski, and Sheldon Solomon.

Basic TMT experiments take the form of making mortality salient to subjects assigned to the experimental group, while making some other topic salient to subjects in the control group. Possible mortality cues include having subjects describe in writing "the emotions that the thought of your own death arouses in you" or subliminally[1] presenting the word "dead". Control cues may prime a totally innocuous concept, such as television, or an aversive but nonlethal concept, such as dental pain or flunking a test. Then the researchers measure subjects' adherence to or defensiveness about supposedly death-denying constructs, such as social groups or religions. Sure enough, mortality salience makes people more clannish: death-primed Christians view Christians more favorably and Jews more negatively (Greenberg et al., 1990), death-primed whites express more positive attitudes towards white racists (Greenberg, Schimel, Martens, Solomon, & Pyszcznyski, 2001), and death-primed Scots judge the English more negatively (Castano, 2004). An example of a subtler mortality-salience effect is provided by Taylor (2012), who found that mortality salience increased preference for TV shows with themes of law and justice, like *Law & Order*. Furthermore, among Taylor's death-primed subjects, watching an episode of *Law & Order* ameliorated a self-enhancing bias observed in subjects who saw no episode or an edited version of the episode in which justice was thwarted. Thus, seeing justice being done seems to comfort death anxiety, and people choose what media to consume accordingly.

[1] Yes, surprisingly enough, subliminal messages can actually work. An example outside of TMT: Karremans, Stroebe, and Claus (2006) got subliminal presentation of the phrase "Lipton Ice" to increase preference for Lipton Ice over mineral water, at least for thirsty subjects. So perhaps the legend of James Vicary (Pratkanis, 1992) was, as a mathematician would say, morally true, after all.

So where do sex and the body come in? You would expect that mortality salience could increase defensiveness about sexual norms just as for any other social norm, as in Rosenblatt, Greenberg, Solomon, Pyszczynski, and Lyon (1989), in which death-primed municipal court judges recommended higher bonds for indicted prostitutes. The thing about the body, though, is that it is itself a reminder of mortality. The fact that our minds are so tightly bound to bodies undermines the symbolic immortality we strive for. We may then be threatened not just by illness and injury but also by *pleasures* of the flesh like food and sex. And the picture is further complicated by how bodies and sex can themselves take on symbolic and therefore terror-management value: think of athletes who strive for an ideal physique, or men who boast of their sexual conquests.

The complex relationship between death and sex in the human mind has been examined primarily by Jamie Goldenberg. To begin with, Study 1 of Goldenberg et al. (1999) found that mortality salience made the "physical aspects" of sex less appealing, in that death-primed subjects gave lower appeal ratings to experiences during sex such as "Having an orgasm" and "Feeling my partner's sweat on my body". Ratings for the "romantic aspects" of sex, like "Blending of selves" and "Expressing love for my partner", were unchanged. Conversely, in Study 2, priming subjects with physical but not romantic aspects increased the accessibility of death (i.e., how readily death-related knowledge was brought to mind), as measured by how subjects filled in word fragments such as "C O F F _ _" that had death-related and non–death-related solutions ("-coffin" versus "coffee"). So it appears that we associate sex with death, and this association is what makes sex potentially unsettling. The significance of the romanticization of sex was best demonstrated by Study 3, which showed that additionally priming subjects with the concept of romantic love removes the increase in death accessibility brought about by a sex prime. So romance can act as a means of whitewashing sexuality: as Goldenberg et al. put it (p. 1,176), "Romantic love transforms sex from an animal act to a symbolic human experience, thereby making it a highly meaningful part of one's cultural worldview and obscuring its threatening link to mortality."

A catch of the effects just described is that they were found only in people relatively high in neuroticism, one of the Big Five personality traits. There are plausible theoretical reasons for this, such as neuroticism either causing or being caused by difficulty with terror management. But the plausibility of TMT as an explanation for large-scale features of human society suffers, since we'd expect that low-neuroticism people have a lot of influence on social norms, too. Fortunately, Goldenberg, Cox, Pyszczynski, Greenberg, and Solomon (2002) were able to find a reduction of the appeal of the physical aspects of sex that *wasn't* influenced by neuroticism, with the help of an additional manipulation: having subjects read an essay that emphasized the similarity of humans to other animals (by saying things like "the boundary between humans and animals is not as great as most people think"). The idea is that maintaining an ideological distinction between humans and animals is another way to defend against the mortality salience of corporeality. When this defense is undermined, even low-neuroticism people can be intimidated by the connection between lust and death.

To extend this thinking to bodily things other than sex, consider Goldenberg et al. (2006). Again, the effects of interest were found only in high-neuroticism people. In Study 2, death-primed subjects spent less time using a foot massager. In Study 1, death-primed subjects lasted for a shorter time in the cold-pressor task, that is, the keeping-your-hand-in-ice-water task, which has a long history of use in experimental psychology as a pain stimulus; in this study, however, subjects "were told that different individuals find the experience 'exhilarating, uncomfortable, pleasurable, or unpleasant.'". The value of this paper is that the dependent measures concern tactile sensations, one pleasurable and one painful, that aren't related to sex and to which few social norms apply.

As an example of how even the physical aspects of sex can manage terror, consider Study 2 of Goldenberg, McCoy, Pyszczynski, Greenberg, and Solomon (2000). Subjects high on a measure of "body esteem" (how positively they viewed their appearance, strength, sensations, etc.) found the physical aspects of sex *more* appealing after a death prime. (Neuroticism wasn't measured.)

Finally, McCallum and McGlone (2011) examined a perhaps more down-to-earth dependent variable: euphemism. Subjects had to write descriptions of nine photographs, supposedly for another subject who would try to answer questions about each image using only the description. Between subjects, the seventh image was randomly assigned to be a picture of dogs urinating, defecating, or copulating. Death-primed subjects were more likely to describe these actions euphemistically.

The moral of the above

That was a lot to digest, so, to review and synthesize: sex, insofar as it is fleshly and creaturely, can be upsetting by its association with mortality. To defend against these mortality concerns, we can distance ourselves from them by euphemizing bodily functions or thinking of ourselves as distinct from animals, or we can whitewash sexuality with socially valued notions like romantic love, or we can try to squeeze some symbolic immortality out of the body itself. While these phenomena are thoroughly entangled with social norms in practice, the core death–body link seems not to require social norms for its existence.

Is terror management responsible for real-life erotophobia?

Altogether, this is a gorgeous theoretical package. The universality of mortality explains the universality of erotophobia, and the diversity of ways in which terror can be managed explains the diversity of sexual rules. The biggest gap is a problem inherent to any attempt to use experimental psychology to explain social trends: external validity. Is the congruence between the laboratory findings of TMT and real-world erotophobia enlightening or misleading? To give a concrete example: we know that sex can arouse mortality concerns, but are mortality concerns really part of why we wear clothes in practice? Another: we know that romance can ease mortality concerns aroused by sexuality, but is this effect really part of why romance is valued to begin with? Such hypotheses about cause and effect in societies as wholes are difficult to test observationally and practically impossible to test experimentally. (Thinking about these things makes one a bit more sympathetic to the methods of sociology, doesn't it? Sociologists seek answers to some very hard questions.) So until some very ambitious studies are run, I have no better answer to such questions than the following: affirmative answers are most consistent with TMT, which is supported by experiment.

Is terror management bad?

It's stupid that we go to such lengths to deny the inevitable. Becker himself argued that the denial of death is responsible for much of the evil in the world: war between ideological factions, for example, may arise because one ideology challenges the soundness of another (e.g., Christian and Islamic beliefs contradict each other) and thus undermines it as a source of symbolic immortality. Frankly, TMT is itself terrifying. However, we should not assume that all behavior that happens to be motivated by mortality concerns is bad. With respect to sex, we'll see in the chapters to come why wariness of human sexuality may be justifiable, and even why it might be wise to dress modestly.

Still, it is reasonable to ask what we can do about whichever aspects of erotophobia we've decided are harmful. (Indeed, as I see it, the primary value of knowing the causes of erotophobia is to help control erotophobia.) I've argued that TMT implies erotophobia in general cannot be vanquished without changing human nature itself. But the diversity we've seen in how people manage terror suggests that, by means of clever social engineering, we may be able to replace people's terror-management strategies with more useful ones, which focus on the actual dangers of sexuality without spilling over into excessive sex-negativity. (For example, imagine if people felt condoms and consent were what made sex palatable.) Obviously, this is easier said than done.

More broadly, I hope you agree that a certain healthy fear of death is a good thing. If we value anything we can do while we're alive, we should value life. Not to mention that terror management may be a key ingredient of human ambition and achievement. Goodness knows that *I'm* trying to get some symbolic immortality out of doing science—that awareness of my own finitude is what motivates me to value my own experiences less than what happens to humanity as a whole. So it's possible to fly from death more prosocially than Voldemort, the *Harry Potter* villain who cast evil spells in the pursuit of immortality.

A final caveat: TMT isn't everything

It has sometimes been suggested that mortality salience is not merely one basic human motive among many, but the most important one, or even the most fundamental one, from which all behavior originates. For example, Greenberg et al. (2008) entertain the notion (although they cite it to Yalom, 1980) that "all psychopathology is (at least in part) the result of ineffective terror management" (p. 128).

I don't like this line of thinking one bit. It smacks of Freud; it's one way that TMT's origin in Becker, a non-scientist, may keep it from developing properly. TMT is a big, powerful theory, but there's hardly evidence that it's equipped to be psychology's theory of everything. Nor should any sane person expect such evidence to arise. One simple reason why: to return to the theme of Goldenberg et al. (2002), human behavior is in many substantial ways similar to the behavior of other animals, but TMT doesn't apply to animals.

Alternative explanations

Let's discuss some candidate alternative causes of erotophobia, not least because terror management may not be the only cause.

My perception is that most writers put the blame for erotophobia on some aspect of culture, such as religion. Along these lines, Fisher et al. (1988) say about erotophobia-the-personality-dimension, "because sexual behavior is inherently rewarding, erotophilia [i.e., low erotophobia] would presumably be the norm were it not for the effects of sex-related punishment" (p. 134). I don't doubt that culture has all kinds of influences on individuals' sexual attitudes, as implied by some of the TMT research. However, the universality of erotophobia raises the question of why so many human cultures happened to become erotophobic before they interacted. So culture isn't an acceptable ultimate explanation.

A disgust theory

One could try to explain erotophobia in terms of disgust. Sex is disgusting because it's unclean. Besides sex being truly unhygenic because of the transmission of bodily fluids like sweat, saliva, and semen, we may mentally associate sex with excretion because the penis excretes urine, the anus excretes feces, and the vagina excretes menses. But we need to overcome this disgust to have sex, so (it appears) evolution has arranged for sexual arousal to dampen disgust reactions, or at least disgust reactions towards sexual stimuli (Stevenson, Case, & Oaten, 2011, observed this in men and Borg & de Jong, 2012, observed it in women). So the overall prediction is that we'll find sexual things disgusting whenever we don't find them arousing. If we combine this line of thinking with the observation I belabored in the chapter on preferences, namely, that sexual preferences are idiosyncratic, it follows that what we find sexually disgusting—our "sexual antipreferences", as it were—should be similarly idiosyncratic. Hypothesize some way by which particular sexual antipreferences could (a) dominate a culture (the same way that some sexual preferences, like a preference for large breasts, dominate cultures) and (b) generalize to negative reactions other than disgust (such as fear), and you have a process for generating kinds of erotophobia as weird as the ones we observe.

I think that this idea is original. There are no direct tests of it. But my reading of the literature (see appendix: `http://arfer.net/w/esa/disgust-theory`) is that support for it is mixed. It doesn't seem equipped to replace TMT any time soon.

Others

I've seen reasonable theories for many classes of the social norms that I've characterized as erotophobic. To wit:

- When resources are scarce, as they have been in most societies, reproduction is risky. If there's too many mouths to feed, someone will starve. Without good contraceptives, regulating coitus is the only reliable way to regulate reproduction. (This is the line of thinking favored by Stearns, 2009.)
- Similarly, one way to avoid STDs is to avoid sex.
- In a society in which paternity is important (e.g., because possessions are inherited patrilineally), paternity has to be known. And the only way to keep track of paternity without paternity testing is to regulate who copulates with whom.
- More generally, one way people might reinforce their social dominance over other people (e.g., men over women, or clergy over laity) is to make the latter follow a lot of unpleasant or degrading rules.
- People may be partly aware of the ways in which sexual stimuli and feelings can have undesirable influences on human behavior (again, see the chapters to come). Rules like nudity bans could be an attempt to minimize such harm. (See DeForest, 2011, for a humorous exposition of this idea.)

While any number of these theories may be right, they're not enough, even as a package. I mean, I can imagine how functional norms, as people lost sight of their purpose over time, could grow into monsters. For example, rules that were intended or that memetically evolved to keep sexual feelings from interfering with cognition may have given birth to a less pragmatic anxiety about sexuality that in turn created Victorianism, even though extreme anxiety about sexuality is a solution worse than the problem. What these theories can't explain, and where TMT shines, is that regulations about sexuality having no obvious function are universal, but obvious fully general anxiety about sexuality is not. (If the horny nude Marquesan girls who swam out to greet sailors (Bolin, 2004) were anxious about sexuality, *they* sure as heck didn't know it.) The regulations imply some kind of crazy unconscious inconsistent-yet-fully-general anxiety about sexuality, which only TMT (and perhaps the disgust theory) can explain. Also, these theories don't enjoy the experimental support of TMT.

Sexuality has many odd and possibly pernicious effects on cognition and decision-making

Experiments have demonstrated a wide variety of ways sexual emotion can influence how we think and decide. Importantly, such findings have been obtained even for non-sexual domains of behavior, and with very weak manipulations of sexual affect, such as the gender of a name. Sexuality then appears to have pervasive, albeit subtle, consequences for human thought. There is no clear overall theme to the findings, except, perhaps, that sexuality often influences us in ways we'd rather not be influenced.

Contents

Effects of sex cues on cognition and decision-making

The idea that sexual motives can perniciously influence one's judgments, decisions, or other cognitive processes is common among laypeople. Particularly well-known is the theme of people making bad decisions about people they're attracted to ("And therefore is winged Cupid painted blind"). Besides the issue of seeing one's beloved through rose-colored glasses, we take it for granted that intense sexual arousal, like any other emotion, can make us impulsive. Ariely and Loewenstein (2006) tested this idea experimentally. Subjects (all men) were asked questions such as "Can you imagine having sex with a 60-year-old woman?", "Would you use a condom even if you were afraid that a woman might change her mind while you went to get it?", and "Would you slip a woman a drug to increase the chance that she would have sex with you?". In one condition, subjects answered these questions while masturbating and looking at nudes. This manipulation succeeded in increasing subjects' stated openness to unconventional, dangerous, or unethical sex.

Part of the title of Ariely and Loewenstein (2006) is "the heat of the moment", and indeed, Ariely and Loewenstein's stated goal was to examine intense sexual arousal ("the heat") and sexual decision-making ("the moment"). But a body of research has accumulated that much weaker manipulations, like showing subjects swimsuit photographs (without having them masturbate at the same time), can be effective, and much more general classes of behavior can be influenced than decisions about sex. This is important for our sexual attitudes. We spend at most a little of our lives having sex or directly pursuing it, so findings limited to such circumstances are accordingly limited in their importance. By contrast, if mild sex cues of the sort we encounter every day, like attractive people, can make a difference for the sort of decisions we make every day, like how long to wait for a bus, this line of research is harder to dismiss. We're left with the impression that sexual affect can have pervasive, albeit subtle, consequences for human thought.

Risk-taking

First of all, Ditto, Pizarro, Epstein, Jacobson, and MacDonald (2006) gave men a role-playing scenario in which a woman was willing to have sex but no condom was available. Subjects who were presented with a video of the scenario instead of a textual description rated the situation as more sexually arousing and were more willing to have sex. Subjects' judgments of danger were not significantly affected.[1] In Blanton and Gerrard (1997), on the other hand, men gave lower estimates of STD risk for more attractive women (so long as extra nondiagnostic information was available, presumably for motivated reasoning). Young and Jordan (2013) had subjects answer a questionnaire that included Facebook photos that were or were not sexually suggestive ("e.g., kissing, flirting with the camera, wearing revealing clothing, groping of other individuals in the photo"; p. 244). Subjects exposed to the suggestive pictures rated themselves as more likely to have unprotected sex, perhaps because they also reported greater "perceived peer prevalence of unprotected sex" (Young & Jordan do not quote the exact questions subjects were asked).[2]

[1] All findings of no significant difference discussed in this book (and, indeed, anywhere) should be interpreted with the statistical fact kept in mind that failure to reject a null hypothesis is not evidence in favor of the null hypothesis. In lay terms: if I fail to get a statistically significant difference between two groups in my study, I'm not justified in concluding that the groups are the same. Thus, a finding of no significant difference has no straightforward interpretation.

[2] There are two other studies in which the sexual manipulation was not directly related to the judgments asked of subjects, but the dependent variable was still the subject's willingness to have sex without a condom. Ebel-Lam, MacDonald, Zanna, and Fong (2009), who had men in the experimental group read a pornographic story with lingerie photos, found an effect of this manipulation combined with alcohol intoxication together, but no main effects, perhaps because the video used for the task was too sexually appealing on its own. Maisto, Palfai, Vanable, Heath, and Woolf-King (2012), who used MSM as subjects and "mildly erotic film clips" as the sexual manipulation, found an effect on subjects' ability to "negotiate sexual situations" but not on willingness to have unprotected sex.

Several studies have examined the evolutionary-psychological idea that men take risks to attract women. Ronay and von Hippel (2010) performed a field experiment in which male skateboarders were watched by a male experimenter or an attractive female experimenter. Subjects were less likely to abort difficult tricks when they were observed by the woman. Lest you think such a result could be explained by some skateboarder stereotype, Dreber, Gerdes, and Gränsmark (2013) analyzed a database of expert chess games. Male players chose riskier opening moves against more attractive female opponents. Interestingly, in neither of these two studies did the increased risk-taking seem to improve overall performance; if anything, performance *decreased* in Dreber et al. (2013). Back in the laboratory, Frankenhuis, Dostsch, Karremans, and Wigboldus (2010), taking a cue from Dutton and Aron (1974), had men play a virtual-reality game in which they crossed "an ominous bridge over a steep valley". Subjects traversed the bridge faster when the experimenter was female and a game character who observed the subject was female (and wore a halter top, compared to the male character's full shirt).

While this peacocking may seem stupid, it isn't mindless: effects on male risk-taking by female observers can be influenced by variables relevant to courtship. For example, in Frankenhuis and Karremans (2012), men read a newspaper article saying that women are attracted to men who are either cautious or take risks. In a subsequent gambling task with a female experimenter, men who were single took riskier bets when the article lauded risk-taking, whereas romantically involved men behaved in the opposite fashion. In Baker and Maner (2009), subjects were male or female, they saw a video of an opposite-sex partner who was either engaged to be married or looking for someone, and they thought their behavior in a gambling task would or would not be observed by the partner. Risk-taking increased only among male subjects who thought they would be observed by a romantically available partner.[3]

[3] Study 1 of Shan et al. (2012) is interesting in that female subjects were found to take *less* risks when observed by men. But I'm nervous about this paper because the data analysis includes a no-observer condition that isn't described in the method section.

In Knutson, Wimmer, Kuhnen, and Winkielman (2008), men saw a photograph and then decided between a one-dollar gamble and ten-cent gamble, each with equal odds of winning and losing. Pictures of "erotic couples" (which, if the figures are honest, consisted of opposite-sex couples kissing with suggestions of nudity but no genitalia shown), compared to pictures of household appliances, made men choose the risky gamble more often. This study is perhaps the clearest demonstration of an effect of sexual stimuli on risk-taking, since the manipulation involved no observer, just an erotic picture, and the dependent variable was simple, non-sexual, and entirely unrelated to the manipulation.

There's even a finding of this kind in animals. In Kavaliers, Choleris, and Colwell (2001) and Kavaliers et al. (2008), male mice became bolder when they were briefly exposed to the odor of a novel estrous female, "bolder" in the sense that they avoided the odor of a predator (a cat or a weasel) less. On the other hand, in Experiment 2 of Godin and Dugatkin (1996), the presence of a female guppy made certain male guppies avoid a predator more.

Intertemporal choice and time perception

Decision-making under uncertainty is the primary economic manifestation of risk-taking. In behavioral economics, a closely related topic is intertemporal choice, the task of deciding between rewards with different delays of receipt. For example, a subject might have to choose whether to get $10 today or $11 tomorrow. Patience is defined using the exchange rates between dollars of reward and days of delay implied by a subject's choices. In Van den Bergh, Dewitte, and Warlop (2008), men who looked at swimsuit photos (compared to landscapes) or inspected brassieres (compared to T-shirts) were less patient in intertemporal-choice tasks. Wilson and Daly (2004) used subjects of both genders and compared attractive to unattractive opposite-sex faces. Men were less patient after seeing the attractive faces; for women, there was a non-significant trend in the same direction.

A lot of variables ought to go into intertemporal choice, from subjects' sensitivity to reward differences to their saving goals, but Kim and Zauberman (2013) found evidence that it is time perception in particular that's affected by sex cues. Men looked at lingerie photos or at pictures of objects like rocks and trees, then expressed the subjective distance they felt from two future times (3 months in the future and 6 months in the future) by adjusting the length of a string. Subjects who saw the lingerie photos judged these distances as longer, and this difference in time perception statistically mediated (i.e., was capable of accounting for) the effect of the manipulation on intertemporal choice. So, this study suggests that sex cues make people less patient because they make delays seem longer.

General cognitive performance

The trope of men getting flustered by women has been experimentally demonstrated. Karremans, Verwijmeren, Pronk, and Reitsma (2009) had subjects perform a fast-paced, cognitively demanding task before and after a short conversation with another person. In Study 1, the task was a 2-back task: subjects watched a stream of letters of the alphabet, presented one at a time, and had to remember whether each letter matched the letter that was presented two trials previously. In Study 2, the task was to watch a stream of words and to indicate whether its meaning was positive or negative if it was white and its color if it was blue or green. Men (but not women) got slower at the task after interacting with a woman (but not a man), and the greater their self-reported concern with impression management during the conversation, the greater the impairment. Nauts, Metzmacher, Verwijmeren, Rommeswinkel, and Karremans (2012) got similar effects with even weaker manipulations. Cognitive performance was measured with the Stroop task, which requires subjects to name the font color a word is printed in even when the word is the name of a different color. In Study 1, being given instructions over instant messages by an experimenter named "Lisa" (but not "Bas", a typical Dutch male name) who supposedly observed the subject during another task worsened men's (but not women's) performance on the Stroop task. In Study 2, merely *expecting* a future task in which the subject would be observed by Danielle (but not Daan) worsened men's (but not women's) performance.

Laier, Schulte, and Brand (2013) had heterosexual-identified men look at 100 photographs of sexual activity, then complete a test of short-term memory. The test had four blocks, each requiring subjects to recognize a different type of photograph: neutral (e.g., people walking in the street), negative (e.g., a mugging), positive (e.g., smiling grandparents), and coitus. Subjects' recognition was impaired in the coitus condition compared to the other three, non-sexual conditions.

Aggression

At odds with the lay notion that sex and violence are opposites (think of the slogan "Make love, not war"), there is some evidence that sex cues make people more aggressive. (For rape and other forms of sexual abuse, see the next chapter.)

Allen, D'Alessio, and Brezgel (1995) conducted a meta-analysis (i.e., a study that tries to quantitatively integrate the findings of a large number of past studies) of experiments in which subjects viewed sexual stimuli of some kind and then had some opportunity to be aggressive. Overall, sexual stimuli, compared to control stimuli, increased aggression. This seemed to hold regardless of (1) the gender of the subject and (2) the gender of the target of the subject's aggression. The type of stimulus, on the other hand, seemed to make a difference. Depictions of nudity without sexual activity actually decreased aggression, whereas depictions of sexual activity, especially violent such depictions, increased aggression.

Ainsworth and Maner (2012) had subjects write about an experience of intense sexual desire or an experience of intense happiness. Then subjects played a game in which they could give their opponent a painful burst of white noise when they won a trial. This game is a common laboratory measure of aggression: for each noise blast, subjects choose the duration and volume, which serve as the dependent variables. Men (but not women) whose ostensible opponent was male and who were less sexually restricted (according to a questionnaire with items like "Sex without love is OK") delivered louder and longer noise blasts when they were sex-primed.[4] Interestingly, the effect of the sex prime disappeared when men were told they'd surpassed their opponent on a few tests (ostensibly tests of intelligence, creativity, and strength).

[4] But also (Ainsworth & Maner, 2012, p. 825):

> We did observe an unpredicted effect of the mating prime among women, such that restricted women became more aggressive toward a male partner. Restricted women tend to avoid intimate encounters with strangers (Simpson & Gangestad, 1991). Thus, one speculative interpretation is that having been primed with mating, restricted women may have viewed their male partner as a potential sexual threat; however, this finding should be interpreted with caution and requires replication.

Griskevicius et al. (2009) asked subjects what they would do if somebody of the same gender "carelessly spills a drink on you and does not apologize". The sexual manipulation, such as it was, had subjects read a story in which they had a romantic and enjoyable date. For female subjects, this prime increased their stated likelihood of being indirectly aggressive against the drink-spiller, as by "talk[ing] behind this person's back". For male subjects, when the drink-spilling was observed by an audience of men (but not of women), the sex prime increased their stated likelihood of being directly aggressive, as by striking the person.

Mussweiler and Förster (2000) had subjects complete word-search puzzles that for the sex-primed group contained some mildly sexual words, such as "Haut" (German for "skin") and "steif" ("stiff"). Men (but not women) asked to throw darts at one of four targets, two of which were faces and two of which were objects, were more likely to choose faces when they were sex-primed. Men (but not women) also chose less-pleasant photographs (e.g., a rotting corpse instead of a puppy) for another participant to look at when they were sex-primed (but mysteriously, and contrary to Ainsworth & Maner, 2012, this worked only when the purported other participant was female). On the other hand, women (but not men) judged a man (but not a woman) described in a vignette as more aggressive when they were sex-primed.

In Roney (2003), men examined some magazine advertisements containing pictures of either young or old female models. The young models increased self-reported feelings of aggression.

Purchases and charity

In a sense, sex sells. Reichert (2002) found that sexual content in advertisements increased stated purchase intentions in most of the studies he reviewed. Perhaps more interesting are two field experiments. Bertrand, Karlan, Mullainathan, Shafir, and Zinman (2010) sent junk mail advertising a loan. Among the many variables manipulated was whether a photograph of a face appeared in the advertisement and the gender and race of the face. A female photo increased the chance of male recipients applying for a loan, whereas women were not significantly affected by the photograph. Landry, Lange, List, Price, and Rupp (2006) had college students solicit donations door-to-door for one Center for Natural Hazards Mitigation Research. Among female solicitors, more attractive solicitors got more people to donate. A similar result was obtained in the lab by Van Vugt and Iredale (2013): men who were observed or thought they were being observed by attractive women (compared to attractive men or no audience) donated more in a public-goods game and volunteered to spend more hours helping a charity. These findings of sex cues increasing generosity, like some of the risk-taking literature discussed earlier and perhaps even findings of increased purchases (using the idea of conspicuous consumption), can be construed as peacocking.

What about women?

In the above literature review, you may have noticed that women appeared as stimuli more often than as subjects. When women were included, the trend was for no significant effect of the manipulation to appear (but see [1]). The overall picture is that male sexuality is more sensitive to these effects. Perhaps this is a consequence of how, in general, men have stronger sexual motivation than women (Baumeister, Catanese, & Vohs, 2001). But other explanations are possible, which brings us to the issue of explaining the existence of these effects to begin with.

Possible explanations

The findings reviewed above, although they share certain themes, are heterogeneous. Besides the wide variety in manipulations and dependent measures I've discussed, I've smoothed over some difficult-to-interpret details: for example, Karremans et al. (2009) found no significant effect of whether subjects were in a relationship, although the findings of Frankenhuis and Karremans (2012) would suggest otherwise. So I deem it likely that there is no single common root cause. Here's a list of candidate explanations, some combination of which will hopefully suffice. As in the chapter on evolution, I won't make an earnest attempt to judge relative credibility because the literature is too fragmented and incomplete for me to do this with much confidence.

• Men are inclined to show off to women in various ways. This inclination is smart enough that it can be influenced by the sexual availability of a woman but dumb enough that it can be triggered at least a little by mere photographs of women.

- Men are inclined to attack other men who threaten their social status. This inclination is triggered by sex cues because competition over women is the reason this inclination exists.

- Sex cues are distracting, attenuating mental abilities such as self-control by consuming some kind of cognitive resource. (Reichert, 2002, found that sex in advertising can backfire by reducing memory for such information as the brand name. Similarly, Bushman, 2005, found that sexual themes in television programs made accompanying ads less effective.) Cognitive resources could be consumed by mindless elaboration of sexual imagery (which phenomenally manifests itself as intrusive sexual thoughts[5]), by the effort of restraining inappropriate sexual behavior (like groping strangers), or by impression management.

- Sex cues trigger a general change in behavior in favor of approach (and action) over avoidance (and restraint).

- Sex cues trigger a general change in cognition in favor of concrete details over abstract generalities (see Förster, Özelsel, & Epstude, 2010, and Epstude & Förster, 2011;[6] but notice that lust and love are often contrasted in these studies, whereas, in this chapter, I've conflated these concepts).

- Sexual stimuli, like anything else that's appealing, can trigger motivated reasoning (see Arfer & Luhmann, 2013, for a case of motivated reasoning induced by a food stimulus).

[5] For evidence that intrusive sexual thoughts are extremely common, at least among young men, see Cameron and Biber (1973). For a review of the idea that intrusive thoughts (as part of a larger construct of craving) can play an influential role in behavior, see Kavanagh, Andrade, and May (2005).

[6] A previous version of this chapter had also cited Förster (2010), but it may have used fake data; see Peeters, Klaassen, and van de Wiel (2015).

Other open questions

Notice that which of the listed explanations are correct isn't the only theoretical tangle of interest here. Some important additional questions are:

- How specific are these effects to sexuality? Are they specific to sexual affect, or are they a general property of arousal,[7] or are they a general property of "basic motivations" like desire for food, or are they a general property of approach motivation?
- What about culture? Even if evolutionary psychologists are right in thinking that the key psychological mechanisms at play are innate, it seems likely that the gender roles and sexual attitudes endorsed by a culture can have some influence of their own.
- What about sexual preferences? For example, would men attracted to men be affected by pictures of men just as most men are affected by pictures of women?
- What about sexual experience? Are more experienced people (people who have sex or masturbate more) sensitized and therefore more vulnerable, or desensitized and therefore less vulnerable?
- What about other individual differences? Do people vary widely in their vulnerability to these effects in ways not predictable by variables like gender and age?

[7] Kim and Zauberman (2013) found the temporal-perception result I discussed earlier for frightening stimuli as well as for sexual stimuli. Now, the subtlety of some of the manipulations I've reviewed might seem to argue against arousal being involved. It's difficult to believe that the men in Mussweiler and Förster (2000) got erections from finding the word "stiff" in a word-search puzzle. But we can take the concept of arousal further if, like Toates (2009), we conceive of arousal as a covert mental construct, like sadness, rather than equating it with physiological variables like penile tumescence and heart rate.

Why should we care about these effects?

So what? What can we glean from this motley bunch of citations? What's the moral of the story?

  Perhaps the most important moral is that sexuality, however subtle, is not trivial. If you don't want to deal with sex or relationships or in-laws, fine, you can abstain; on the other hand, there's no clear way to entirely avoid these many strange influences of sexual motivation. Think of the effects in terms of "mental contamination", which Wilson and Brekke (1994) define as "the process whereby a person has an unwanted judgment, emotion, or behavior because of mental processing that is unconscious or uncontrollable. By unwanted, we mean that the person making the judgment would prefer not to be influenced in the way he or she was..." (p. 117) Psychological research tells us that our lives are teeming with mental contamination of all sorts. As Wilson and Brekke point out, correcting for mental contamination is no small feat: one must be aware that the contamination exists in the first place, motivated to correct for it, cognizant of the direction and magnitude of the bias (or else one might overcompensate, or compensate in the wrong direction), and able to change one's behavior appropriately. The weakness of human introspection (Nisbett & Wilson, 1977) implies that this is, in practice, impossible. And thinking that mental contamination poses no threat to you might make the problem worse. In Study 3 of Nordgren, van Harreveld, and van der Pligt (2009), smokers led to believe they had better self-control accepted greater temptation in a self-control game (for a greater monetary reward) and were more likely to lose the game. Study 4, a nonexperimental 4-month longitudinal study, examined smokers who'd just quit. Smokers with greater self-control beliefs didn't avoid temptation as much and were more likely to relapse. I'd speculate that, similarly, trivializing mental contamination could make you complacent about it, making you more likely to expose yourself to sources of it and thereby aggravate the harm.

  The worst-case possibility can be caricatured as follows: sexual feelin's make you careless, impatient, stupid, and violent, and the most you can do about it is avoid sex cues, and good luck with *that* in the world we live in.

  But actually, before we even try to avoid or compensate for

these influences, we might ask whether they are, in fact, bad. After all, whereas some of the effects seem clearly undesirable, like increased aggression, and some are of dubious value, like altered time perception, some seem beneficial, like increased generosity. The truth is that while psychology experiments are excellent for identifying the motivational forces underlying behavior and what directions those forces push people in, they're poorly suited to quantifying the real-life consequences of those forces, and such quantification is what we need for real-life decision-making.

Imagine, for example, that the executives at some business, upset with the underrepresentation of women among their employees, decide to recruit women more aggressively, and they succeed in balancing the sex ratio. We can expect that this change will make the male employees a bit more aggressive and a bit more generous. But how will these changes compare to each other in magnitude? And is it possible that the aggression could be ultimately good for the business (by making the men more effective salesmen) and the generosity be ultimately bad (by making the men too eager to make sacrifices)? And how will the effects of the women on the men compare to the effects of the men on the women? If the executives were deciding whether to recruit more women to begin with, and they wanted to meaningfully apply the research I've discussed in this chapter, they'd need to be able to estimate answers to these questions (not to mention weigh these concerns properly against all other relevant concerns, from ethics to tax consequences). And in order to make such estimates, they'd need much fancier research than what exists now. For starters, they'd need explicit statistical models of the effects of arbitrary sex cues on arbitrary behavior. That's the kind of sophistication that I doubt psychology will achieve in my lifetime.

Anyway, the point of this thought experiment is: it's not totally clear whether the odd consequences of sexual motivation are good or bad for the human race, and it won't be totally clear anytime soon. In the meantime, I have a few suggestions. Don't hang up swimsuit calendars in offices. Dress modestly in public. And be wary of the idea that sex is necessarily good.

Sexual abuse is universal and dangerous

Sexual activity to which one partner does not consent is seen in all human cultures and many non-human species. Its frequency can differ dramatically between cultures, but it is very common in the United States, especially between acquaintances and romantic partners and in its milder forms. Rape is associated with even more psychological damage to the victim than non-sexual traumas, and even sexual abuse short of rape is damaging. The evidence of damage from child sexual abuse, however, is less clear than the evidence of damage from abuse of adults. Precisely what makes sexual abuse aversive during the event and traumatizing afterwards is unclear.

Contents

Introduction

In this chapter, I will examine sexual abuse from the victim's perspective: who gets abused, and what does abuse do to victims mentally? The next chapter examines possible causes of abuse, and thus concerns the abuser more than the victim. Throughout both chapters, I will examine various popular beliefs and stereotypes about sexual abuse.

Preliminaries

Talking about rape is complicated by ambiguity about the meaning of the word "rape". Often, it includes only particular sexual acts. In this book, I'll use a liberal definition: "rape" will mean any case of non-consensual (i.e., unwanted) sex (and by "sex", I mean, as usual, partnered genital or anal contact). I will use "sexual abuse" or just "abuse" (non-sexual abuse will not be covered) to mean *any* non-consensual act that involves sexuality. So, all rape counts as sexual abuse, but shouting eroticized comments at strangers is an example of sexual abuse that isn't rape (because it isn't sex). My concern in this book is more with sexual abuse as a whole than rape in particular, but I'll be discussing rape a lot because it has a much deeper associated research literature than less concrete forms of sexual abuse.

"Sexual violence" is an increasingly common term for what I call "sexual abuse". I think that's misleading, because violence and nonconsent are distinct and each is worth understanding in its relationship to sexuality. Sexual acts can be violent but consensual, as in sadomasochism, or non-violent but non-consensual, like a manager demanding sexual favors from his employee. See the previous two chapters for research on the connection between sex and violence.[1] On the other hand, I'll avoid the term "sexual harassment" because it is often meant to include only behavior that occurs in the context of work or school.

[1] Possibly the appeal of the term "violence" is just that it sounds harmful, since people talking about sexual abuse are usually trying to get the public to agree that sexual abuse is a problem. The OED's entry for the word "violence" quotes a 1984 *Daily Telegraph* article as saying "much violence was done to the word violence, which it appears can be used to describe almost anything you do not care for".

Of course, in order to distinguish sexual abuse from non-abusive sexual behavior, we need to define consent. And here's the real trouble with that: we speak as if consent were an unambiguous discrete entity, and the law tends to treat it as such. In reality, many different constraints can affect people's sexual decisions, from physical force to employment risk to intoxication to ignorance or inexperience to intellectual disability to social norms to the other person's feelings—not to mention that animals, too, make sexual decisions, and clearly not in exactly the same way humans do. It is debatable which combinations and degrees of constraint qualify as consent and which as coercion. We can create bright-line rules to make the rule of law possible, but there are many scenarios in which people can reasonably disagree as to whether a sexual act is abusive. Is it sexual abuse to beg and plead with one's partner for sex? What about implicit exchanges of sex for other favors (like a fancy dinner or household chores)? What about threatening to leave the relationship? Untangling such difficult ethical issues is not what I intend to do here; the point is just to demonstrate that hard-and-fast rules distinguishing abuse from non-abuse (particularly, rape from non-rape) will necessarily be misleading, and therefore should be avoided in empirical (as opposed to legal) discourse.

It is important to distinguish consenting from desiring and liking. Consent is what we usually mean by the term "want" (e.g., "I want to go home" means "I'd go home if I could choose to do so"), but one can also "want" something in the sense of feeling desire for it without consenting. Hence, sexual desire does not equal consent; for all sorts of reasons, one could choose not to have sex despite experiencing desire for it, or, conversely, one could choose to have sex without desire (e.g., because there's nothing good on TV). As Muehlenhard and Peterson (2005) point out, ambivalence (at a more individual scale than I discussed in the earlier chapter on erotophobia) is underappreciated in sex research. And people of both sexes can be sexually aroused and reach orgasm during obviously involuntary sex (Levin & van Berlo, 2004; Pari, 2013). Similarly, enjoyment of a sexual act isn't the same thing as desiring it (Loewenstein, 2009) or consenting to it.

The topic of sexual abuse, even more than the rest of sexuality, is thoroughly intertwined with ethical and political issues. These concerns are an obstacle to understanding the empirical phenomena of sexual abuse. They threaten to create prejudice in the conduct and interpretation of research. In particular, there seems to be a latent requirement to emphasize how bad sexual abuse is —"bad" in the senses of both "morally reprehensible" and "damaging to victims". But if we want to prevent and treat sexual abuse as well as possible, we should try to understand it scientifically as well as we can, and that requires resisting these biases. Openly allowing ethical concerns to bias our thinking about empirical matters would be shortsighted and self-defeating.

Universality

Sometimes, rape is described as unnatural. Brownmiller (1975), for example, wrote: "...rape is a deliberate distortion of the primal act of sexual intercourse—male joining with female in mutual consent..." (p. 369). Actually, rape is probably universal in human civilization, and appears in a wide variety of animal species. In a word, rape is natural—just like many of the other possibly distasteful, but more ethical, sexual activities discussed in earlier chapters.

Palmer (1989) examined claims that rape, in the narrow sense of men forcing or coercing women into coitus, never occurs in each of 17 societies. He found contradictory evidence for many of these societies and at best sparse supporting evidence for the remainder. Rozée (1993) found rape in every one of 35 cultures she surveyed, including in her definition of rape, unlike past investigators, culturally sanctioned acts like marital or ceremonial rape. At the same time, it's worth noting Palmer's observation that punishment or censure for at least some forms of rape also appears universal. That is, there is no clear example of a culture that condones all forms of rape.

Also, despite the absence of truly rape-free cultures, there can be dramatic differences between cultures in how common or socially acceptable rape is. On one end of the spectrum are some striking examples cited by Sanday (1981). There have existed societies in which men boast of making their new wives unable to walk after their wedding night (the Gusii of Kenya), girls are gang-raped as part of a marital initiation ceremony (the Arunta and Ilpirra of Australia; Baldwin & Gillen, 1899), or men in general are permitted to rape women at will (the Marshallese). On the other end of the spectrum are societies whose ethnographers, or whose ethnographers' informants, state that rape simply does not occur, as in the case of the Lesu of Papua New Guinea and the Tewa of New Mexico (Palmer, 1989). Even if we accept Palmer's assertion that we should expect stronger evidence than an ethnographer's or informant's denial for the total absence of rape in a culture, we are obliged to believe that rape (in the narrow sense) among peoples such as the Lesu and Tewa is particularly rare. The cross-cultural variability of rape with different genders or different sexual acts, and of milder forms of sexual abuse, is an open question.

Lalumière, Harris, Quinsey, and Rice (2005b) provide a detailed review of rape among animals. In some species, such as the fly *Sepsis cynipsea*, goldenrod soldier beetles, and northern elephant seals,[2] females visibly resist every or nearly every attempt at coitus. In others, such as migratory grasshoppers, mallards, and Bornean orangutans, females welcome some coitus attempts and resist others. Animal rape can be quite violent: male elephant seals, for example, being about five times as large as females, hit and bite their victims and may injure females or pups in the course of a rape. There are even cases of animals raping humans: Galdikas (1995) observed several instances involving juvenile male Bornean orangutans. Galdikas describes some orangutans masturbating themselves against humans (p. 130, 137), one attempting to insert its penis in a man's ear (p. 130), and one forcing coitus on a woman (p. 293–294; this is the only incident for which Galdikas uses the word "rape"). However, Lalumière et al. (2005b) found no cases of female animals forcing males into coitus, making this the only category of sexual behavior I know of that is unique to humans.

[2] A previous version of this chapter included bottlenose dolphins in this list, on the basis of a discussion in Lalumière et al. (2005b), p. 38. However, one of the same dolphin researchers whose work Lalumière et al. cite, Richard C. Connor, made an argument to the contrary 15 years later in an interview for, of all publications, *PolitiFact* (Carroll, 2016). The *PolitiFact* article concludes that dolphin rape is "just a myth". I haven't looked closely at this literature, so feel free to draw your own conclusions.

Some writers reject any comparison of rape among animals to rape among humans. For example, Brownmiller (2000) and Cowan (2009), which are both reviews of evolutionary-psychological books on rape, mock the included discussions of scorpionflies and snow geese, respectively, apparently on the argument that scorpionflies and snow geese do not have the social phenomena that these authors prefer to study as causes of rape. Lalumière et al. (2005b) is one of the works being reviewed, but even it shies away from calling forced sex among animals "rape", preferring "forced copulation" and "resisted mating". In general, whereas many authors say it is unfair to anthropomorphize animal rape by calling it "rape", I think that this is putting the burden of proof on the wrong side of the issue. Only if we have good reason to think that animal rape is uninformative to the study of human rape should we dismiss it, and only if calling animal rape "rape" is somehow misleading should we characterize it as "not really" rape. Otherwise, we're unnecessarily prejudicing how we think about these issues.

One difficulty with the idea of animal rape is that, legally speaking, animals can't consent to anything. I see this as an example of why consent should be thought of as a nebulous entity arising from the combination of many constraints rather than an all-or-nothing phenomenon. Even if animals do not have the full decision-making and communicative capacities of humans, we can still examine how well an animal's expressed sexual choices are respected by conspecifics.

Frequency and demographics

As people are increasingly realizing in this age of Bill Cosby, Brock Turner, and Donald Trump, sexual abuse is very common, at least in the contemporary United States.[3] A recent national survey produced the following figures (Black et al., 2011):

[3] Yes, I, too, have been sexually abused, albeit mildly. When I was thirteen (in 2002 or 2003), one of my classmates would proposition me crudely and giggle when I cringed or gave her a look of horror. Once, she stroked my arm seductively. After I complained to one of the school's staff, she apologized to me and never bothered me again. If only most sexual abuse was so easily stopped. Incidentally, I was bullied a great deal at the same school in non-sexual ways and my many complaints about those incidents achieved nothing, but I suppose bullying is its own vast social problem that's distinct from sexual abuse.

- About 1 in 3 women and 1 in 8 men have had "non-contact unwanted sexual experiences".
- About 1 in 4 women and 1 in 9 men have "experienced unwanted sexual contact" short of penetration.
- About 1 in 4 women and 1 in 71 men have been forcibly penetrated, subject to attempted forcible penetration, or penetrated while intoxicated.

- About 1 in 21 men have been forced to penetrate someone else.

Rates can be even higher in special social contexts. For example, Sadler, Booth, Cook, and Doebbeling (2003) found that 399 of 505 female veterans of the American military (79%) had been sexually abused during their time in the military.

Basile (2002), using data from a 1997 nationally representative poll of women, found that 34% "had sex with a husband or intimate partner when they really did not want to". Respondents were also asked whether they'd had such unwanted sex in a variety of circumstances, ranging from ambiguously coercive ("when you thought he expected sex from you in return for certain actions, such as spending money on you for a gift or taking you out for a nice dinner") to forceful ("after he used physical force on you in order to have sex"). In general, less coercive forms were more common.

Brousseau, Bergeron, Hébert, and McDuff (2011) examined sexual abuse in Canadian opposite-sex couples. Both partners of every included couple were asked both about what their partner had done to them and what they had done to their partner. Of 222 couples, 45% reported the woman being victimized, 30% reported the man being victimized, and 20% reported mutual victimization (also included in the former two percentages). Hickson et al. (1994) interviewed 930 British men who were ("in general") gay-identified. About 1 in 4 (28%) had been raped. The rapists were male in 96% of cases.

Notice that while, consistent with stereotype, most victims are women and most abusers are men, there are still substantial numbers of female abusers and male victims. One can find statements suggesting that nearly all rapists are men (e.g., Black et al., 2011, say "For female rape victims, 98.1% reported only male perpetrators"); an important reason is that the word "rape" is often restricted to penetration by the abuser, which excludes, for example, the abuser forcing the victim to penetrate. Krahé, Waizenhöfer, and Möller (2003) is a rare study of women as sexual abusers of men. Krahé et al. had 248 German women complete questionnaires. 4% admitted to attempts to forcibly rape a man. 3% had verbally pressured a man into sex and 8% had attempted to exploit some incapacitated state (such as drunkenness). Abusive oral sex or coitus was less common than "sexual touch (kissing/petting)". This said, a meta-analysis (i.e., a study that tries to quantitatively integrate the findings of a large number of past studies) by Cortoni, Hanson, and Coache (2010) found that less than 3% of female sex offenders commit another sexual offense after their first conviction; this recidivism rate is substantially lower than that of non-sexual offenses among women or sexual offenses among men.

In the popular imagination, "rape" is often taken to imply the sudden violent assault of a woman by a strange man. As we have seen, less intense and forceful forms of abuse are more common, and the genders are often different. Moreover, only a minority of rapes are committed by strangers; acquaintances and romantic partners (including spouses) are more often the culprits. Martin, Taft, and Resick (2007), from a review of other studies, state "marital rape is the most common form of rape" (p. 336). In Black et al. (2011), a partner was the abuser for 51% of female victims and 45% of male victims of rape involving penetration. An acquaintance was the abuser for respectively 41% and 53%. A stranger, by contrast, was the abuser for respectively 14% and 8%. Strangers were more likely to be abusers for less severe forms of abuse (for example, 51% of non-contact abuse to women was committed by strangers), but there were still substantial numbers of partner and acquaintance abusers.

Traditionally, writers on rape have focused on the most headline-worthy sorts of rape: young, vulnerable women savaged by such frightening men as lunatics, slavers, and soldiers. Bryden and Grier (2011) observe that Brownmiller (1975), the most influential book on rape yet written, devotes many of its pages to racially and politically charged rape during wars and revolutions and few to acquaintance rape and date rape, while the clinical psychologists who were the primary authorities on rape before Brownmiller's book focused on incarcerated sex offenders. Headline-worthy rape is indeed worth our attention, but we must not lose sight of ordinary, everyday sexual abuse (rape or otherwise), the sorts of abuse that are responsible for the startlingly high abuse rates I've cited. Sexual abuse is very common, it happens to ordinary people, and ordinary people perpetuate it—and yet, it still devastates its victims. I expect we will need to understand sexual abuse in this its most basic form to understand how it fits into human sexuality as a whole.

Sexual abuse of young children seems to be much rarer than abuse of adolescents and adults. Finkelhor, Hammer, and Sedlak (2008) discuss a nationally representative sample of children and their caretakers. They found that 1 in 900 children under 12 years old and 1 in 1,600 children under 9 years old have been sexually abused.[4] I would tell you something about the gender ratio, but it's hard to find research reports on abuse of prepubescents as opposed to all children under 18. (The gender ratio for all children seems to be similar to that for adults.)

[4] I calculated these figures from Table 2 of Finkelhor et al. (2008) as (123 + 98 + 305) / ((.33 + .17 + .17) * 701727) and (123 + 98) / ((.33 + .17) * 701727).

Consequences

In agreement with the common view of rape as an especially horrific crime, research suggests not only that rape is mentally damaging to victims, but that it is on average *more* mentally damaging than other kinds of trauma. Kilpatrick et al. (1989) and Boudreaux, Kilpatrick, Resnick, Best, and Saunders (1998) found that among women, rape, compared to other crimes, was more strongly associated with symptoms of (respectively) post-traumatic stress disorder (PTSD) and other mental illnesses such as major depression and agoraphobia. Similarly, Moor and Farchi (2011) found in a sample of 304 people (including both men and women) that forcible rape, compared to non-sexual traumas such as "sudden loss of a loved one" and "involvement in a serious car accident", was more strongly associated with PTSD and with endorsement of self-blame statements such as "I got what I deserved" and "I should have been more cautious". Vrana and Lauterbach (1994) also found in a sample of 440 college students that sexual abuse was more associated with PTSD, anxiety, and depression than traumas such as combat and natural disasters.

As one would expect, less severe forms of victimization seem to be associated with less mental damage. For example, Boudreaux et al. (1998) found stronger associations between completed rape and mental illness than attempted rape and mental illness. Importantly, however, milder forms of sexual abuse, including non-contact abuse, are still related to mental illness. Petersen and Hyde (2013) asked 5th-grade children (aged about 10) about "nine potentially offensive behaviors" that same-age peers had done to them, ranging from "spread sexual rumors about you" to "touched, grabbed, or pinched you in a sexual way". Among girls, the sum of these behaviors that had occurred to subjects and that they rated as "somewhat upsetting" or "very upsetting" was positively associated with eating disorders four years later. Fitzgerald, Drasgow, Hulin, Gelfand, and Magley (1997) surveyed 473 female employees of a utility company about abuse they had experienced in the workplace such as "crude sexual remarks", "staring, leering at you", and "repeated requests for drinks, dinner, despite rejection" (items quoted from Fitzgerald, Gelfand, & Drasgow, 1995). Such abuse was associated with PTSD symptoms and a measure of general mental distress (such as anxiety and depression). In summary, it is not justified to trivialize milder forms of sexual abuse. In fact, if milder forms of sexual abuse are more common, the full human cost of milder forms may well equal or exceed the cost of forcible rape.

Consequences of child abuse

If the public views rape of adults as evil, it views rape of children as unconscionable. Surprisingly, then, empirical evidence of the damage of child abuse is less clear than the damage of adult abuse. A meta-analysis by Rind, Tromovitch, and Bauserman (1998) concluded that child abuse "does not produce pervasive and intensely negative effects regardless of gender" (p. 42); in particular, boys seem less likely to be harmed. (So popularly and politically controversial was this conclusion that the US Congress officially condemned the American Psychological Association for publishing the article; Garrison & Kobor, 2002. But this article does not actually argue that adult–child sex is acceptable; Hunter, 2008, is an example of one that does.) A nationally representative survey by Briere and Elliott (2003), on the other hand, found that child abuse is indeed associated with long-term symptomatology.

A possible obstacle to research on child abuse is that operational definitions of child abuse tend to be wider than those of adult abuse. In particular, whereas research on adult abuse usually only considers victims who say they did not want the sexual experience, research on child abuse tends to ignore this variable. Child–adult sex is often regarded as necessarily abusive, whatever the child's feelings on the matter, on the argument that a child's agreement to sex does not suffice for consent—because of the adult's social power over the child, because of the child's relative lack of knowledge about sex, or because of children's lower overall cognitive ability. (People may also be unaware that some kinds of sexual behavior with same-age children are common in prepubescents, as discussed in the chapter on preferences, leading them to believe that prepubescents can never feel genuine sexual interest.) Research on child abuse might be improved by inclusion of the child's views on the matter. In particular, I expect that child-abuse victims who do not agree to the sex at the time of the original event are no less likely to be harmed than abused adults.

Hines and Finkelhor (2007) review the sparse literature on sex between adolescents and adults that the adolescent describes as voluntary. There seem to be substantial numbers of adolescents who perceive these experiences as positive and substantial numbers who perceive them as negative, although frequencies are hard to estimate. Evidence on the distinct question of whether adolescents are actually harmed by these relationships is also mixed.

Associates of symptomatology

Intuitively, we think of psychological trauma as the lingering damage of the original, acutely aversive stressor, similarly to how a bodily injury can be painful initially and disabling in the long term. A difficulty of applying this idea to sexual abuse, however, is that isn't obvious why sexual abuse is aversive to begin with (in cases of abuse that do not involve other stressors, such as violence or the threat of violence). Violence is aversive because it's physically painful, and theft is aversive because it takes away possessions we want or need, but why is sexual abuse aversive? The question is all the more worth our attention if sexual abuse is *more* aversive than other traumas, which is suggested by how, as just discussed, it tends to have more negative mental effects. Unfortunately, this question has not received much empirical attention, perhaps because empirical researchers tend not to be interested in phenomenology (i.e., people's subjective experience). We can approach the matter, however, by reviewing research on how characteristics of abuse events or victims' responses to them influence the mental consequences for victims.

Victims of rape, as of other traumas, sometimes report feeling numb or detached ("as though you were in a dream or watching a movie or play"; Griffin, Resick, & Mechanic, 1997, p. 1087) during the trauma. This experience is called "dissociation". Such an emotional detachment from a traumatic event might be expected to reduce suffering during the event and hence subsequent mental damage. However, dissociation during rape is associated with worse, not better, consequences for the victim. Griffin et al. (1997), for example, found that women who reported more dissociation during a rape were higher in PTSD symptoms and depression. On the other hand, confusingly, subjective distress during a rape is also positively related to symptomatology. Feinstein, Humphreys, Bovin, Marx, and Resick (2011) found that peritraumatic (i.e., during-the-event) fear was associated with PTSD symptomatology, and Girelli, Resick, Marhoefer-Dvorak, and Hutter (1986) found that the more subjects rated they had peritraumatically been "afraid for my life and safety" and "extremely upset, crying", the greater their fear and anxiety afterwards.

Here are some other characteristics of victims' reactions to rape that are associated with symptomatology. In Moor and Farchi (2011), discussed earlier, self-blame was associated with PTSD among victims of several traumas but particularly among rape victims. Gutner, Rizvi, Monson, and Resick (2006) examined coping strategies used by women who had been raped or violently assaulted. Subjects who engaged in more wishful thinking or social withdrawal from friends and family had more PTSD symptomatology.

In lieu of more research on this subject, I would like to add some speculation.

First, recall that, although the terror of rape and the pleasure of consensual sex may seem antagonistic, victims may experience arousal and orgasm during rape (Levin & van Berlo, 2004). This suggests it should be possible to feel sexual pleasure during rape, even contemporaneously with much less pleasant emotions. (If this sounds impossible, imagine drowning in a vat of honey. While you are experiencing the agony of drowning, you can also taste the honey's sweetness, cold comfort that it is.) I hypothesize that, far from providing some sort of meager compensation for the suffering of rape (as suggested by Clayton Williams's infamous remark "If it's inevitable, just relax and enjoy it."; Associated Press, 1990), sexual pleasure will make things worse, peritraumatically or in the long term. Awareness that one has obtained sexual gratification out of the event may make one feel more blameworthy for the event and more confused about one's other, negative reactions. I know of a single case study (Coelho, Rodrigues, Andersen, Tufik, & Hachul, 2013) reporting an abuse victim's feelings of guilt for pleasure she had experienced during the abuse.

Second, recall from the chapter on ambivalence the experimental evidence that people are inherently afraid of sexuality because of its connection with death, and social constructs such as idealized romantic love serve to buffer people against this fear. When a person is sexually abused, they have an experience that is sexually charged but to which whitewashing social ideals, such as idealized romantic love, are more difficult to apply than usual. (To apply them, in fact, might contaminate them with the trauma of rape and thereby reduce their efficacy for everyday terror management in the future.) The victim is in a sense disillusioned as the creaturely nature of sexuality is bared to them. This sudden, involuntary confrontation of what people unconsciously dread about sexuality is probably not conducive to mental health.

Finally, it might be enlightening to conduct cross-cultural research on the consequences of sexual abuse for victims. In cultures in which rape is very common or institutionalized, will victims be not as badly affected (perhaps because their worldview is not much changed by being raped) or even worse affected (perhaps because they feel even more helpless)? More generally, how much are cultural forces responsible for victims' reactions to rape?

Sexual abuse has both sexual and non-sexual causes

The idea that sexual abuse is an act of desperation by sexually deprived men is not supported. However, sexual abuse does seem to be motivated by sexual interest in the victim and by less selective sexual preferences (specifically, a tendency not to be sexually inhibited by expressions of non-consent). In terms of non-sexual causes, abuse seems to share the causes of non-sexual crimes and antisocial behavior, and it is enabled by cultural environments in which women are less powerful and by sexist attitudes. What all this means for prevention and treatment is unclear.

N.B. See the section "Preliminaries" in the previous chapter for definitions of terms like "abuse" and "consent".

Contents

Introduction

One of the most important questions about sexual abuse—particularly about the relationship between sexual abuse and sexuality—is the cause of sexual abuse. Here I will examine several possible causes, which vary in their plausibility and amount of relevant research. This is by no means an exhaustive review (Tharp et al., 2013, list 67 distinct constructs that have been studied as associates of sexual abuse). The focus is on sexuality-related causes, with additional treatment of two causes unrelated to sexuality that to me seem particularly important.

As I mentioned in the preface, the best kind of research design for making causal inferences is a true experiment, in which subjects are randomly assigned to different values of the supposed causal variable. But obvious ethical concerns make true experiments difficult or impossible to design for many hypotheses related to sexual abuse, so we'll have to rely on non-experimental research for most of this chapter.

Sexual deprivation

There are a number of arguments people have put forth that somehow pin the blame on insufficient sexual expression (well, insufficient *non-abusive* sexual expression).

A direct form of this argument relies upon the construct of sex drive. The thinking goes like this: if people have a hunger-like drive to seek sexual stimulation that increases over time until sufficient stimulation is acquired, then a particularly desperate person might resort to rape, just as starving people may resort to cannibalism. But I argued against the existence of a sex drive in the chapter on practices.

I don't doubt the existence of sexual desire itself, of course. And so one could argue instead that abuse results merely from intense sexual desire without a better target. But what could be more convenient than masturbation? And many petabytes of pornography are readily available on the Internet. Even the difficulty, expense, and risk involved in getting a prostitute in places where prostitution is illegal is arguably more convenient than rape. One needs to believe one of the following:

1. The rapist's sexual desire is less diffuse and more targeted at the rape victim. (In this case, the argument has ceased to be about general sexual deprivation and thus no longer falls under this heading.)
2. The rapist's sexual desire is diffuse enough not to be specific to the victim, but still picky enough to demand real

sex, so masturbation and pornography don't suffice.[1]

3. Rape is still somehow the path of least resistance (perhaps because, in some cultures, it is more socially acceptable than masturbation!).

[1] This is reminiscent of a concept of sex drive that Apfelbaum (1984) mocks:

> Freud may even have had a hidden assumption that "excitation" must build up in order to create an adequate discharge [of sexual urges], and thus the "masturbator" who discharges "the smallest quantity of excitation" may be getting a "faulty" result.[...] If this indeed was Freud's assumption, these vesicular nerve endings begin to look unusually demanding. They may well want foreplay and even romance.

Whatever the exact form of the deprivation argument, we can examine the general notion that people's sexual inhibition or lack of sexual experience makes them more likely to commit abuse.

On the subject of sexual experience, Lalumière, Harris, Quinsey, and Rice (2005a) list several studies in which admissions of sexual abuse were associated with greater sexual experience and greater sexual promiscuity, particularly casual sex (e.g., Dean & Malamuth, 1997; Christopher, Owens, & Stecker, 1993; Lalumière & Quinsey, 1996; Lalumière, Chalmers, Quinsey, & Seto, 1996; Senn, Desmarais, Verberg, & Wood, 2000; there is also a finding of this kind in Peterson, Janssen, & Heiman, 2010). In Lalumière et al.'s (2005a) words (p. 76):

> This literature provides no support for the often-proposed idea that men who do not have access to consensual sexual partners are more likely than other men to engage in rape: Sexually coercive men, as a group, appear to be more, rather than less, sexually experienced than other men. Sexually coercive men are not just more sexually experienced; they also seek greater partner variety and more casual sex than other men. Indeed, Lalumière et al. (1996) found that a measure of preference for partner variety and casu-

> al sex was related to a history of sexual coercion
> even when a composite measure of sexual experience
> was statistically controlled.

So, that idea is not tenable.

As for sexual inhibition, Peterson et al. (2010) conducted an online survey of 1,240 heterosexual-identified men. Subjects completed two scales of sexual inhibition, one measuring inhibition due to the threat of performance failure (e.g., "When I have a distracting thought, I easily lose my erection") and one measuring inhibition due to consequences (e.g., "If I realize there is a risk of catching a sexually transmitted disease, I am unlikely to stay sexually aroused"). The latter kind of inhibition was *negatively* associated with sexual abuse. That is, men who said they were less likely to have sex due to undesirable consequences of sex admitted to committing less abuse. On the other hand, inhibition due to threat of performance failure was positively related to abuse. Peterson et al. (2010) suggest this may be because men with erection problems want to rush their partners into sex before they go flaccid, or because men avoid the threat of rejection that causes their performance difficulties by coercing their partner into sex. Similarly, Carvalho, Quinta-Gomes, and Nobre (2013) found that male Portuguese college students who had sexually abused others had more erectile and orgasmic difficulties. Perhaps contrary to Peterson et al. (2010), Carvalho et al. (2013) also found that abusers were higher in "sexual embarrassment" (e.g., "I find it difficult to sexually let myself go in front of the other person"). Finally, Jones, Rossman, Wynn, and Ostovar (2010) surveyed 569 female rape victims and found that 8% said their assailants had had erectile impotence. I'm not sure what figures to compare this to, but 8% sounds high.

The grandest form of the deprivation argument is that however things work at the individual level, restrictive sexual attitudes inherent in society ("sexual repression") tend to increase rape. But cross-cultural research has produced no support for this idea. Sanday (1981) found no significant correlations between the frequency of rape in a society and four variables she related to sexual repression: the duration of the postpartum sex taboo, attitude towards premarital sex, men's age at marriage, and the number of "taboos reflecting male avoidance of sexuality". I preformed my own analysis of this kind (see appendix: http://arfer.net/w/esa/

rapepred) using about 65 societies coded as part of the Standard Cross-Cultural Sample. Similarly to Sanday, I failed to predict rape using the frequency of premarital sex or using attitudes about children's sexual expression.

In summary, the deprivation argument has not fared well empirically. Abusers have more, not less, sex than non-abusers, and cross-culturally, sex-negative cultural attitudes are not clearly related to rape. Only some kinds of sexual inhibition at the individual level, related to performance anxiety and embarrassment, seem to be associated with rape, and it is not obvious how to interpret these relationships. I don't know of anybody, lay or scholarly, who's argued that performance anxiety is an important cause of sexual abuse.

Sexual desire

At the opposite extreme from the claim that sexual deprivation causes rape is the claim that sexual desire plays no causal role in rape at all. In fact, some writers have said that rape isn't sex, or that it shouldn't be called "sex". Strongly anti–rape-as-sex ideologies like these were mainstream in psychology in the 1970s and 1980s (Palmer, 1988; Bryden & Grier, 2011) and remain a frequent sight in feminist writing today (enter "rape isn't sex" into your favorite Web search engine for plenty of fresh examples in non-academic feminist writing).[2]

[2] Brownmiller (1975) is sometimes credited for making this idea mainstream, but she doesn't seem to believe it herself. Although she clearly rejects arguments in terms of sex drive or sexual deprivation ("...rape is not a crime of irrational, impulsive, uncontrollable lust, but is a deliberate, hostile, violent act of degradation and possession on the part of the would-be conqueror, designed to intimidate and inspire fear...", p. 361), she devotes a lot of space to the eroticization of rape in fiction and the news, suggesting some role for sexual affect in rape.

But there is a variety of evidence of the role of sexual affect in rape. This is not to say that sexual desire or sexual attraction suffice for rape (that would tend towards the deprivation argument I just rejected), or even that they are strictly necessary. I am only making the weak claim that sexual desire is a common motive for sexual abuse, at least for men's rape of women, in the same simplistic way that desire for goods is a common motive for theft. This idea is in addition to any more complex roles of sexual affect in abuse.

One piece of evidence is the literature on rapists' sexual experience and interest in casual sex discussed in the previous section. This implies that rapists indeed have the motive of sexual gratification, with a hint that they aren't demanding of intimacy in their sexual relationships. Then there are experiments suggesting that sexual stimuli or sexual arousal increase men's chances of committing sexual abuse. In Ariely and Loewenstein (2006) (discussed earlier in the chapter on cognition), men who were masturbating and looking at nudes while they answered a questionnaire rated themselves as more likely to commit abuse such as "slip[ping] a woman a drug to increase the chance that she would have sex with you". In Loewenstein, Nagin, and Paternoster (1997), men who looked at nudes were more likely to say they would try to coax a woman who says "she thinks she is not interested in having sex" into undressing. Bouffard (2002) and Bouffard and Miller (2014), using the same hypothetical scenario as Loewenstein et al. (1997), found (mostly) no significant effect of the sexual-stimulus condition on stated likelihood of abuse, but self-reported sexual arousal was associated with abuse.

Goetz, Easton, Lewis, and Buss (2012) found evidence that men are particularly attracted to women who appear vulnerable to being sexually exploited. Men looked at a large variety of pictures of (clothed) women and rated the women on various characteristics. Higher ratings of attractiveness were associated with higher ratings of abuse vulnerability (e.g., "How easy would it be for a man to sexually assault this woman?") and 19 of 22 visual cues rated by separate judges (e.g., "flirty", "revealing clothing", "intoxicated", "sleepy") that correlated with vulnerability ratings also correlated with attractiveness in the same direction. So, far from men not being sexually interested in rape, it seems that perceived ease of victimizing a woman is part of what determines how attractive she is.

See below for research on the effects of the victim's sexual attractiveness.

Finally, it should be pointed out that claims that rape is a form of violence *instead of* sex are wrongheaded in assuming that sex and violence are antithetical. Experiments I reviewed in the chapter on cognition demonstrate that sexual stimuli can make people more aggressive.

See Palmer (1988) for additional nit-picking on the issue of whether rape is sexually motivated.

Sexual preferences

Some writers have suggested that rapists are not merely especially interested in sex, but have a particular sexual interest in rape, or some other quirk of their sexual preferences that makes rape especially appealing to them.

This sort of question is a natural opportunity for the use of phallometry, the measurement of penile erection, usually by fitting a strain gauge around the subject's penis and recording changes in circumference. Greater increases in penis size are interpreted as more sexual interest. The value of phallometry, in theory, is that it is more difficult for men to control their erectile response than to lie about their subjectively experienced sexual preferences, and deceit is an obvious concern when we are trying to measure such socially charged variables such as sexual interest in children (subjects may even fear, e.g., that parole could be denied on the basis of their sexual preferences). This is not to say that phallometry is immune to fakery, but steps can be taken to reduce subjects' voluntary control over their erections, as by requiring them to press a button every time they hear a sex-related word in a story (Seto, 2008, p. 34). Phallometry does have the weakness of being inapplicable to female subjects. Measurement of genital arousal in women is possible, but genital arousal is not as clearly related to self-reported subjective arousal in women as in men (Chivers, Seto, Lalumière, Laan, & Grimbos, 2010), suggesting trouble for use of such measurement to assess sexual preferences.

Phallometric studies have indeed found that sexual abusers, compared to non-abusers, have greater erectile response to abuse-relevant stimuli. For example, a meta-analysis by Hall, Shondrick, and Hirschman (1993) found that abusers of women exhibit "slightly more" arousal to stimuli depicting rape than comparison subjects. A meta-analysis by Lalumière and Quinsey (1994), using men known to have forcibly raped an adolescent or adult woman, found a larger effect in the same direction. Lalumière, Quinsey, Harris, Rice, and Trautrimas (2003), in a review of five studies conducted since these two meta-analyses, argued that the conclusion of rapists having greater erectile response to rape than non-rapists did was upheld. Similarly, studies of child abusers (Freund & Blanchard, 1989; Blanchard et al., 2006; Barbaree & Marshall, 1989) find that child abusers have greater erectile response to pictures of nude prepubescents or stories of adult–child sex than comparison subjects (either nonoffenders or offenders against adult women).

A potential problem with the phallometric literature is the emphasis on documented and often convicted sex offenders as opposed to ordinary people, who, I argued in the previous chapter, are responsible for the majority of abuse incidents. But there have been a handful of studies on people drawn from ordinary subject pools (e.g., college undergraduates) who admit to abusing or being willing to abuse, and the findings are generally congruent (Malamuth, 1986; Lohr, Adams, & Davis, 1997; Bernat, Calhoun, & Adams, 1999). Also, in keeping with the lower rate of abuse victimization among prepubescent children than adults, substantial sexual interest in prepubescents seems to be uncommon; Seto (2008) (p. 6–8), from a review of the few relevant studies, estimates that less than 5% of men, and still less women, have such interest. A small degree of arousal to prepubescent girls, greater than that to males of any age, may be reasonably common in men (e.g., Hall, Hirschman, & Oliver, 1995).

You may now be suspecting that abusers' lust for abusive sex is a chief cause of abuse. But the evidence I've discussed so far is also compatible with another theme. The question, to be precise, is whether abusers prefer abusing others to consensual sex (perhaps also having little to no interest in consensual sex), or whether they are merely *less deterred* by lack of consent than non-abusers while still preferring consensual sex. This latter idea, which I think can be credited to Blader and Marshall (1989), appears to be better supported. For example, in Bernat et al. (1999) and Harris, Lalumière, Seto, Rice, and Chaplin (2012), abusers, like non-abusers, had fuller erections to consensual than non-consensual stimuli. The latter study, which orthogonally manipulated violent, non-consensual, and sexual themes in the stories read to subjects, found similarly that abusers' arousal was inhibited by violence and injury, albeit less so than in non-abusers. Outside phallometry, Heilbrun and Loftus (1986) had male undergraduates rate the sexual attractiveness of women posing six facial expressions of emotion. The bulk of subjects (44 out of 50) found happiness most attractive, but abusers found fear, anger, disgust, and sadness less unattractive than non-abusers did.

There are some studies (e.g., 9 of the 16 reviewed by Lalumière & Quinsey, 1994) that do find greater erectile response among rapists to rape than consensual stimuli. Without doing my own meta-analysis, my impression is that this is not the rule, and I would expect it to be even less common among abusive ordinary people than documented sex offenders. Unfortunately, a lot of phallometric studies (e.g., Freund & Blanchard, 1989; Blanchard et al., 2006) only report data that has been processed and standardized in such a way that positive interest in abuse and reduced inhibition can't be distinguished. There seems to be more faith in the positive-interest idea for the case of child abusers than adult abusers (see, e.g., the discussion section of Harris et al., 2012), but I don't see a lot of evidence for it. In Barbaree and Marshall (1989), for example, only 35% of subjects who had abused unrelated children, and no subjects who had abused their own children, had a phallometric profile suggesting a preference for pre-pubescents over adults.

I described earlier how abusers are more sexually promiscuous in general. This dovetails with the idea that they have a greater breadth of sexual interest than non-abusers rather than their interest requiring abusive themes. On that note, consider Seto and Lalumière (2010), a meta-analysis of studies comparing male adolescent sex offenders to male adolescents who had committed other crimes. The biggest estimated difference, although there were relatively few studies on the topic, was in "atypical sexual interests", a heterogeneous group of variables ranging from interest in rape to general hypersexuality to interest in cross-dressing. Not mentioned in Seto and Lalumière (2010) is that Daleiden, Kaufman, Hilliker, and O'Neil (1998) found that abusers, compared to non-abusers, were more likely to identify as bisexual and less to identify as heterosexual.

Sex-related features of the victim

It's hard to say which I've seen more of, claims that women's sexual attractiveness, particularly their choice of clothing, can provoke abuse, or denials of the same. There is plenty of research on people's beliefs about this issue (e.g., Cassidy & Hurell, 1995; DeJong,

1999; Kanekar & Kolsawalla, 1980), and Burt (1980) includes "When women go around braless or wearing short skirts and tight tops, they are just asking for trouble." as a rape myth. But, infuriatingly, there is little research to help settle the question of which side is actually right. And the issue has been clouded by confusion of the empirical question of the effects of victims' behavior with the ethical question of whether victims deserve any blame for their own rape. In my view, mere revealing clothing or seductive behavior does not merit blame for being raped, any more than wearing jewelry in a dangerous neighborhood merits blame for being robbed of it.

I know of only one study that has examined the empirical question regarding clothing. Flowe, Stewart, Sleath, and Palmer (2011) had 157 heterosexual-identified men imagine they were in a sexual encounter with a woman whose photograph they saw. The randomly-assigned photograph had the woman wearing either revealing or non-revealing clothing. Subjects read through a 29-line story in which the encounter got progressively closer to coitus but also the woman evinced progressively less consent. At each line, subjects chose whether to continue or to stop. 22% of subjects shown revealing clothing chose to continue even after the woman said outright she wanted to stop, compared to 4% of subjects shown conservative clothing. Thus this experiment supports the notion that revealing clothing increases one's odds of being raped.

Relatedly, but less directly, Guéguen (2011) conducted a field study of men who approached a female confederate in a bar who wore either sexually suggestive or conservative clothing. Men were quicker to approach the suggestively clad confederate and rated themselves as more likely to successfully obtain a date and more likely to have sex on the first date. Also recall that Goetz et al. (2012) found that men rated women who wore revealing clothing in a photograph as both more attractive and easier to "sexually assault". If more suggestive clothing makes men perceive women as more sexually receptive or easier to rape, perhaps it will also make them more likely to attempt date rape.

Another relevant finding is that women at more conventionally attractive ages (young adulthood and adolescence) are more likely to be raped. This theme is perhaps most clearly demonstrated by the studies of robbery reports conducted by Felson and Krohn (1990) and Felson and Cundiff (2012). The closer female victims of robbery were to young adulthood, the likelier they were to be raped by the robber.

I know of a single study on the issue of whether people rated as more attractive by independent judges are more likely to be sexually abused. It obtained mixed results. Petersen and Hyde (2009) asked children in 5th, 7th, and 9th grade (aged about 10, 12, and 14 respectively) about their history of sexual abuse (at the hands of other children, not adults) and also rated their visual attractiveness. Attractiveness was associated with being sexually abused by other children among 7th-grade girls, but significant results were not found for 7th-grade boys or any students in 5th or 9th grade.

The popular belief that more sexually active or promiscuous women are more likely to be abused is supported by a wealth of studies. Greene and Navarro (1998), in a survey of 274 undergraduate women, found that being sexually abused was positively associated with number of sex partners and positive attitudes towards sexual pleasure. Testa and Dermen (1999), in a community sample of 198 women, found that being abused was positively related to a history of casual sex. Kennair and Bendixen (2012), in a representative sample of 1,199 Norwegian high school students, found that being abused was positively related to causal sex and unrestricted sexual attitudes for both boys and girls. Finally, Vicary, Klingaman, and Harkness (1995), in a sample of 112 adolescent girls, found that those who had been abused described themselves as more sexually active and had more sexually active female friends.

Unfortunately, these sexual-activity results are made much more difficult to interpret by a measurement problem. In all four of the studies just cited, the measure of how much sexual abuse victims had experienced was based on a count of incidents or a time-based rate. The problem with such a measure for comparing the rates of abuse against subjects with differing numbers of sex partners or rates of sexual activity is that a great deal of abuse is committed by dates and significant others, and it stands to reason that the more people you date, the greater the odds that at least one of your dates will abuse you. What is needed is some kind of per-partner or per-encounter measure of being abused.

Antisociality

This book is about sexuality, so I've spent quite a few words in the last few sections talking about causes of sexual abuse that are specific to sexual affect. But now, almost as a revenge of the rape-is-n't-sex idea, consider sexual abuse as just another crime. Or, more correctly, think of it as antisocial behavior. Although the word "antisocial" is often mistakenly used to mean something like "reclusive", in psychology, its meaning is closer to "evil". Antisocial behavior is behavior that is selfish and harmful to other people or destructive to human welfare; antisociality is a tendency to commit antisocial acts. Now, some writers (e.g., Lalumière et al., 2005a) make strong claims about antisociality as a reified personality trait that is caused by individual differences in genetics and in turn causes antisocial behavior such as rape. I will avoid such difficult questions about unobservable constructs and instead make the weak claim that sexual abuse is largely caused by whatever causes other antisocial behavior; in other words, in some respects, sexual abuse is just another crime.

Sexual abuse can be construed as a typical crime as follows. Think of a crime as a thing somebody does that gives them some personal benefit at the expense of somebody else's interests. If Bob steals Alice's wallet, for example, he has enriched himself while impoverishing Alice. If Bob strikes Alice during a heated argument, he has gratified his anger at her while causing her pain. And if Bob rapes Alice, he has gotten sexual gratification while causing her distress. This perspective suggests that a sexual motive is (usually) necessary for sexual abuse, but far from sufficient. The causal factor of interest is not Bob's desire to have sex with Alice—people want to have sex with other people, and yet refrain from abusing them, all the time!—but Bob's willingness to do something antisocial. The question is not why rapists are *motivated* to rape but why they're *willing* to do it.

The frequency and demographics figures for abuse that I discussed earlier turn out not to be too specific to abuse. Just as most abusers are men, most criminals are men: "male criminal participation in serious crimes at any age greatly exceeds that of females, regardless of source of data, crime type, level of involvement, or measure of participation" (Blumstein, Cohen, Roth, & Visher, 1986, p. 40). This may be related to how males are more physically aggressive than females across cultures and primate species (Fry, 1998); across human cultures, boys are more physically aggressive than girls even in prepubescence (Best & Williams, 1997, p. 185). Victimization rates also seem roughly similar for sexual and non-sexual crimes. Black et al. (2011) found that about 1 in 4 women and 1 in 7 men were violently assaulted by a partner; compare this to 1 in 4 women and 1 in 9 men "experienc[ing] unwanted sexual contact" short of penetration in the same study. Vrana and Lauterbach (1994) found that of 440 undergraduates, 13% had experienced "sexual assault/rape" and 10% had experienced "violent crime". Dansky, Brewerton, Kilpatrick, and O'Neil (1997), in a nationally representative sample of women, found that 14% had experienced forcible rape and 9% had experienced non-sexual violent assault.[3] Writers who report substantially different rates for violent crime and sexual abuse tend to give the former the larger figure (Koppel, 1987; Truman & Planty, 2012). Perhaps, overall, it is less correct to say the US has a rape crisis than that it has a crime crisis. Finally, in general, rape rates are positively correlated with the rates of other crimes over time and across cultures (Lalumière et al., 2005a, p. 62). Sanday (1981), using a large sample of cultures, found that the degree of interpersonal violence in a culture correlated positively (+.47) with its rape frequency.

[3] These percentages are row margins of Table 1 of Dansky et al. (1997).

There is also an association between sexual abusiveness and overall antisociality at the individual level, at least for males. A literature review by Tharp et al. (2013) found that aggression and lack of empathy were generally associated with sexual abuse. Voller, Long, and Aosved (2009) asked male college students how appealing they found committing sexual abuse as well as committing non-sexual crimes, such as bank robbery. Interest in non-sexual crimes was positively related both to interest in sexual abuse and a history of actual abusiveness. Lalumière and Quinsey (1996), in a study of 99 young men, found that antisocial attitudes were positively related to both stated likelihood of abusing and stated history of abusing. Lalumière et al. (1996), using a sample of 156 male university students, also found the relationship between antisocial attitudes and history of abusing was positive in direction, albeit nonsignificant. Calhoun, Bernat, Clum, and Frame (1997) found another relationship of this kind among 65 young adult males in rural Georgia.

Regarding child abuse, a meta-analysis by Whitaker et al. (2008) concluded that risk factors for abusing children and adults are largely the same.

Sexism

Feminists have long argued that rape is enabled by, or even helps to maintain (Brownmiller, 1975), society-wide woman-oppressing attitudes and male dominance over women. Cross-cultural research indeed supports an association between the status of women and rape (men's rape of women, at least). Sanday (1981) found that the presence of an "Ideology of Male Toughness" correlated positively (+.42) with rape. Again, I did my own analyses (see appendix: http://arfer.net/w/esa/rapepred) with about 45 societies from the Standard Cross-Cultural Sample. I found that an "Ideology of Male Superiority" predicts more rape. Using another variable, I found that among cultures with a belief that women are generally inferior to men, rape is likely to be reasonably common or institutionalized. Among cultures without such a belief, on the other hand, rape rates vary more widely. Schlegel and Barry (1987) found an association between rape and a more indirect indicator of the status of women. In a sample of 30 preindustrial societies, the greater women's contribution to subsistence (which one could construe as a measure of economic importance), the less likely rape was.

Possibly the most common kind of psychological study of rape is one in which people's self-reported beliefs and attitudes related to gender and sex are related to willingness to abuse or a history of abusing. There are so many such studies that I will defer to Tharp et al.'s (2013) review (p. 24–25). Among the beliefs and attitudes that have been studied are endorsement of "rape myths" (beliefs or attitudes specifically concerning rape), hostility towards women, adversarial or exploitative views of sexual relationships, endorsement of traditional gender roles, and focus on maintaining one's own masculinity. Overall, these variables have been found to be positively related to reported abusiveness. In summary, anti-feminist beliefs and attitudes are associated with sexual abuse.

A word about rape myths. In lay language, the term "myth" often means claims of fact that are known to be false, such as "Most rape victims are raped by strangers." But included in the beliefs assessed by scales of rape-myth endorsement, specifically the original scale created by Burt (1980) that seems to have remained the most popular one, one also finds ethical claims (e.g., "Women who get raped while hitchhiking get what they deserve.") and claims of fact that are certainly not known to be true but I do not know of empirical evidence falsifying them (e.g., "Many women have an unconscious wish to be raped, and may then unconsciously set up a situation in which they are likely to be attacked."). Perhaps the problem is just that "myth" is the wrong word, but there is also a suggestion that it may be helpful to use tests that are more homogeneous, such as one measuring explicit victim-blaming and another measuring beliefs about who gets raped. As Lonsway and Fitzgerald (1994) observe, there is widespread disagreement among researchers about what exactly rape myths are and how to measure them.

This literature focuses on male abuse of women, since that's what the theory is all about. Studies concerning other gender combinations are sparse, but Tharp et al. (2013) point out that Lacasse and Mendelson (2007) found that female sexual abusers endorsed traditional gender roles *less* than female controls. I'm not sure what to make of this.

Conclusion and a caveat

The studies reviewed here suggest that sexual abuse is due to a variety of causes. Abuse is motivated by sexual interest in the victim and less selective sexual preferences (specifically, a tendency not to be sexually inhibited by expressions of non-consent), and enabled by antisocial tendencies and sexist or woman-disempowering culture and attitudes. Notice that explanations favored by Darwinists as well as feminists have been supported, showing that the ideological struggle between these factions is something of a false dichotomy (Vandermassen, 2011, explains how the gap can be further bridged at a theoretical level). The only major category of explanation I have rejected is explanations in terms of the rapist's sexual deprivation.

By and large, this is good news. Humanity seems on the way to understanding sexual abuse at a scientific level. As for the practical matter of preventing and treating abuse, though, this research is less helpful than it might seem. As Bryden and Grier (2011) observe (p. 264–273), theorists' policy proposals have rarely been original enough to require the theory as inspiration, and the policies themselves have rarely fared well empirically. The biggest contribution to rape policy has been by feminists, who have done a great deal to open the public's eyes to the ubiquity and danger of abuse, as well as reduce victim-blaming. But these benefits have come more from consciousness-raising about demographic facts of abuse and winning sympathy for victims than from popularizing feminist theory about the causes of abuse.

To prevent and treat sexual abuse, it is not enough to understand its causes. We will need to empirically examine actual policies and therapies. Such research is more difficult, more expensive, and more potentially harmful to participants than basic research, but it's what we need to counter abuse.

Epilogue

> There's something here to offend just about every-
> one. —A reviewer of a submitted journal article,
> quoted in Quinsey (2008), p. 80

In the preface of this book, I mentioned that "I'm more sex-negative than sex-positive". The contents of this book, particularly the
later chapters, show that a certain degree of antagonism or suspi-
cion towards human sexual emotion is justifiable, if not required.
We have seen that not only are humans innately predisposed to
find sexual matters somewhat upsetting, sexual stimuli have various strange effects on people's thinking and decision-making, sexual desire provides motivation for an enormous amount of sexual
abuse, and victims of severe sexual abuse are psychologically
harmed even more than victims of non-sexual traumas. Culture can
ameliorate or aggravate these problems but not, so far as we have
seen, eliminate them. Clearly, human sexuality is not all rainbows
and sunshine.

But it's also possible to be too sex-negative. First of all, don't
forget those earlier chapters. A wide variety of sexual practices and
preferences are common, and in most cases, we have no good reason to think they do any harm, outside of harm induced by a culture that irrationally condemns them. And we have seen that the
traditional view that sexuality is for reproduction alone faces many
challenges. To see sex-negativity in its purest and most extreme
form, though, you'd have to look at the antisexual community, a
loose coalition of people on the Internet that I considered myself
part of for a few years. In particular, I participated in a Web forum
for Anglophone antisexuals that no longer exists today. There is no
research on antisexuals, so I will describe my own perceptions.

Self-described antisexuals have never been very numerous or
ideologically homogeneous. The solidarity of the movement has
been hindered by the language divide between English and Russian
speakers as well as by an ambivalent relationship with the asexual
movement (which, unlike the antisexual movement, has lately
rapidly increased in visibility and perceived legitimacy by the public, partly by ostracizing antisexuals; it is not a mistake that AVEN
policy is adamantly sex-positive despite how not all AVENites are

sex-positive themselves). The central idea of antisexualism is that sexual affect and sexual behavior are destructive to personal health and social harmony. Antisexuals frequently characterize sex as a distraction or addiction. Although they may happen to agree with religious prescriptions, their arguments are secular. They frequently, although not invariably, feel no sexual attraction or desire. They are almost always celibate.

Initially, I was excited to learn that the antisexual community existed. Here, for the first time, were people who shared my antagonism towards sexuality itself, as opposed to some particular sexual preference. Over time, as I discussed with other antisexuals the ideas that eventually led to this book, I began to both moderate my own views on sexuality and realize that antisexuals were not interested in moderation. While I liked and agreed with a number of individual antisexuals, the community as a whole turned out to be too dogmatically sex-negative for my tastes. There is too much emphasis on portraying sexuality in a bad light by any means handy rather than trying to understand, characterize, and control it. Antisexuals see sexuality less as a force of nature to be coped with than a social evil to be quashed. Now, I am convinced that if we want to best limit whatever harm sexuality may do, we need to understand it realistically, not demonize it. We need empirical sexual attitudes.

On that note, I want to return to a very general theme I touched on in the preface. Sexuality is something people have strong opinions about, although they are unaware of both the empirical research that has been conducted and how much research is left to be done to answer the questions that they think they already know the answers to. But sexuality is not the only topic for which this is the case. Political controversies of all sorts rage on in the United States and around the world with no consideration of empirical research. Moral and philosophical arguments are tossed about as if everybody already knew the facts, and yet, by and large, we don't know the facts. We are obliged to make countless uninformed decisions. We try to circumnavigate the globe in a rowboat without a map.

Awareness of our own ignorance is the first step towards fixing it.

Bibliography

If you try to visit a URL and find that the referenced page is gone or has moved, use the Wayback Machine (http://web.archive.org) to find an archived version.

Abramson, P. R. (1973). The relationship of the frequency of masturbation to several aspects of personality and behavior. *Journal of Sex Research, 9*(2), 132–142. doi:10.1080/00224497309550788

Ainsworth, S. E., & Maner, J. K. (2012). Sex begets violence: Mating motives, social dominance, and physical aggression in men. *Journal of Personality and Social Psychology, 103*(5), 819–829. doi:10.1037/a0029428

Allen, M., D'Alessio, D., & Brezgel, K. (1995). A meta-analysis summarizing the effects of pornography II: Aggression after exposure. *Human Communication Research, 22*(2), 258–283. doi:10.1111/j.1468-2958.1995.tb00368.x

Anderson, C. A., Shibuya, A., Ihori, N., Swing, E. L., Bushman, B. J., Sakamoto, A., ... Saleem, M. (2010). Violent video game effects on aggression, empathy, and prosocial behavior in Eastern and Western countries: A meta-analytic review. *Psychological Bulletin, 136*, 151–173. doi:10.1037/a0018251

Apfelbaum, B. (1984, November). *Sexual reality and how we dismiss it.* Paper presented at the meeting of the American Association of the Advancement of Science, San Francisco State University, San Francisco, CA. Retrieved from https://web.archive.org/web/20010627190317/http://www.bapfelbaumphd.com/Sexual_Reality.html

Arfer, K. B. (2011). *Vicarious restraint.* Retrieved from http://arfer.net/w/vicarious-restraint

Arfer, K. B. (2012). *Cheese.* Unpublished raw data. Retrieved from http://arfer.net/projects/cheese

Arfer, K. B., & Luhmann, C. C. (2013). *Cake that good is risky to refuse: Motivated reasoning in motivationally charged decisions.* Retrieved from http://arfer.net/projects/csearch/cake_paper.odt

Arfer, K. B., & Luhmann, C. C. (2015). The predictive accuracy of intertemporal-choice models. *British Journal of Mathematical and Statistical Psychology, 68*(2), 326–341. doi:10.1111/bmsp.12049. Retrieved from http://arfer.net/projects/builder/paper

Ariely, D., & Loewenstein, G. (2006). The heat of the moment: The effect of sexual arousal on sexual decision making. *Journal of Behavioral Decision Making, 19*(2), 87–98. doi:10.1002/bdm.501

Ariely, D., Loewenstein, G., & Prelec, D. (2006). Tom Sawyer and the construction of value. *Journal of Economic Behavior and Organization, 60*, 1–10. doi:10.1016/j.jebo.2004.10.003

Armour, R. A. (2001). *Gods and myths of ancient Egypt.* Cairo, Egypt: American University in Cairo Press.

Associated Press. (1990, March 26). Texas candidate's comment about rape causes a furor. *The New York Times.* Retrieved from http://www.nytimes.com/1990/03/26/us/texas-candidate-s-comment-about-rape-causes-a-furor.html

Aversa, A., Mazzilli, F., Rossi, T., Delfino, M., Isidori, A. M., & Fabbri, A. (2000). Effects of sildenafil (Viagra) administration on seminal parameters and post-ejaculatory refractory time in normal males. *Human Reproduction, 15*(1), 131–134. doi:10.1093/humrep/15.1.131

Baker, M. D., Jr., & Maner, J. K. (2009). Male risk-taking as a context-sensitive signaling device. *Journal of Experimental Social Psychology, 45*(5), 1136–1139. doi:10.1016/j.jesp.2009.06.006

Baker, R. R., & Bellis, M. A. (1993). Human sperm competition: Ejaculate adjustment by males and the function of masturbation. *Animal Behaviour, 46*(5), 861–885. doi:10.1006/anbe.1993.1271

Baldwin, S., & Gillen, F. J. (1899). Certain ceremonies concerned with marriage together with a discussion regarding the same. In *The native tribes of central Australia.* Oxford, England: Macmillan. Retrieved from http://ebooks.adelaide.edu.au/s/spencer/baldwin/s74n/chapter3.html

Barbaree, H. E., & Marshall, W. L. (1989). Erectile responses among heterosexual child molesters, father-daughter incest offenders, and matched non-offenders: Five distinct age preference profiles. *Canadian Journal of Behavioural Science, 21*(1), 70–82. doi:10.1037/h0079791

Barrett, L. F. (2012). Emotions are real. *Emotion, 12*(3), 413–429. doi:10.1037/a0027555

Basile, K. C. (2002). Prevalence of wife rape and other intimate partner sexual coercion in a nationally representative sample of women. *Violence and Victims, 17*(5), 511–524. doi:10.1891/vivi.17.5.511.33717

Baumeister, R. F., Catanese, K. R., & Vohs, K. D. (2001). Is there a gender difference in strength of sex drive? Theoretical views, conceptual distinctions, and a review of relevant evidence. *Personality and Social Psychology Review, 5*(3), 242–273. doi:10.1207/S15327957PSPR0503_5

Bernat, J. A., Calhoun, K. S., & Adams, H. E. (1999). Sexually aggressive and nonaggressive men: Sexual arousal and judgments in response to acquaintance rape and consensual analogues. *Journal of Abnormal Psychology, 108*(4), 662–673. doi:10.1037/0021-843X.108.4.662

Bertrand, M., Karlan, D. S., Mullainathan, S., Shafir, E., & Zinman, J. (2010). What's advertising content worth? Evidence from a consumer credit marketing field experiment. *Quarterly Journal of Economics, 125*(1), 263–306. doi:10.1162/qjec.2010.125.1.263

Best, D. L., & Williams, J. E. (1997). Sex, gender, and culture. In J. W. Berry, M. H. Segall, & Ç. Kağıtçıbaşı (Eds.), *Handbook of cross-cultural psychology: Social behavior and applications* (Vol. 3, pp. 163–212). Boston, MA: Allyn and Bacon. ISBN 0-205-16074-3.

Black, M. C., Basile, K. C., Breiding, M. J., Smith, S. G., Walters, M. L., Merrick, M. T., ... Stevens, M. R. (2011). *The National Intimate Partner and Sexual Violence Survey (NISVS): 2010 summary report.* Atlanta, GA: National Center for Injury Prevention and Control, Centers for Disease Control and Prevention. Retrieved from http://www.cdc.gov/

violenceprevention/pdf/nisvs_report2010-a.pdf

Blader, J. C., & Marshall, W. L. (1989). Is assessment of sexual arousal in rapists worthwhile? A critique of current methods and the development of a response compatibility approach. *Clinical Psychology Review, 9*(5), 569–587. doi:10.1016/0272-7358(89)90012-3

Blanchard, R., & Hucker, S. J. (1991). Age, transvestism, bondage, and concurrent paraphilic activities in 117 fatal cases of autoerotic asphyxia. *British Journal of Psychiatry, 159*, 371–377. doi:10.1192/bjp. 159.3.371

Blanchard, R., Kuban, M. E., Blak, T., Cantor, J. M., Klassen, P., & Dickey, R. (2006). Phallometric comparison of pedophilic interest in nonadmitting sexual offenders against stepdaughters, biological daughters, other biologically related girls, and unrelated girls. *Sexual Abuse, 18*(1), 1–14. doi:10.1177/107906320601800101

Blanton, H., & Gerrard, M. (1997). Effect of sexual motivation on men's risk perception for sexually transmitted disease: There must be 50 ways to justify a lover. *Health Psychology, 16*(4), 374–379. doi: 10.1037/0278-6133.16.4.374

Blumstein, A., Cohen, J., Roth, J. A., & Visher, C. A. (Eds.). (1986). *Criminal careers and "career criminals"* (Vol. 1). Washington, D.C.: National Academy Press. ISBN 978-0-309-03684-9.

Bockting, W. (2003). United States of America — Autoerotic behaviors and patterns — Research update. In R. T. Francoeur & R. J. Noonan (Eds.), *The Continuum complete international encyclopedia of sexuality*. New York, NY: Continuum. Retrieved from https://kinseyinstitute.org/ pdf/ccies-unitedstates-part1.pdf

Bolin, A. (2004). French Polynesia. In R. T. Francoeur & R. J. Noonan (Eds.), *The Continuum complete international encyclopedia of sexuality*. New York, NY: Continuum. Retrieved from https:// kinseyinstitute.org/pdf/ccies-frenchpolynesia.pdf

Borg, C., & de Jong, P. J. (2012). Feelings of disgust and disgust-induced avoidance weaken following induced sexual arousal in women. *PLOS ONE*. doi:10.1371/journal.pone.0044111

Boudreaux, E., Kilpatrick, D. G., Resnick, H. S., Best, C. L., & Saunders, B. E. (1998). Criminal victimization, posttraumatic stress disorder and comorbid psychopathology among a community sample of women. *Journal of Traumatic Stress, 11*(4), 665–678. doi:10.1023/A:1024437215004

Bouffard, J. A. (2002). The influence of emotion on rational decision making in sexual aggression. *Journal of Criminal Justice, 30*(2), 121–134. doi: 10.1016/S0047-2352(01)00130-1

Bouffard, J. A., & Miller, H. A. (2014). The role of sexual arousal and overperception of sexual intent within the decision to engage in sexual coercion. *Journal of Interpersonal Violence, 29*(11), 1967–1986. doi: 10.1177/0886260513515950

Briere, J., & Elliott, D. M. (2003). Prevalence and psychological sequelae of self-reported childhood physical and sexual abuse in a general population sample of men and women. *Child Abuse and Neglect, 27*(10), 1205–1222. doi:10.1016/j.chiabu.2003.09.008

Brody, S. (2006). Penile-vaginal intercourse is better: Evidence trumps ideology. *Sexual and Relationship Therapy, 21*(4), 393–403. doi: 10.1080/14681990600891427

Brousseau, M. M., Bergeron, S., Hébert, M., & McDuff, P. (2011). Sexual coercion victimization and perpetration in heterosexual couples: A dyadic investigation. *Archives of Sexual Behavior, 40*(2), 363–372. doi: 10.1007/s10508-010-9617-0

Brownmiller, S. (1975). *Against our will: Men, women, and rape.* New York, NY: Simon and Schuster. ISBN 0-671-22062-4.

Brownmiller, S. (2000, February 23). *Thornhill: Rape on the brain.* Retrieved from http://www.susanbrownmiller.com/susanbrownmiller/html/review-thornhill.html

Bruce, H. M. (1959). An exteroceptive block to pregnancy in the mouse. *Nature, 184*, 105. doi:10.1038/184105a0

Bryden, D. P., & Grier, M. M. (2011). The search for rapists' "real" motives. *Journal of Criminal Law and Criminology, 101*(1), 171–278.

Burt, M. R. (1980). Cultural myths and supports for rape. *Journal of Personality and Social Psychology, 38*(2), 217–230. doi: 10.1037/0022-3514.38.2.217

Bushman, B. J. (2005). Violence and sex in television programs do not sell products in advertisements. *Psychological Science, 16*(9), 702–708. doi: 10.1111/j.1467-9280.2005.01599.x

Butler, K. (2006, March 7). Many couples must negotiate terms of *Brokeback* marriages. *The New York Times.* Retrieved from http://www.nytimes.com/2006/03/07/health/07broke.html

Calhoun, K. S., Bernat, J. A., Clum, G. A., & Frame, C. L. (1997). Sexual coercion and attraction to sexual aggression in a community sample of young men. *Journal of Interpersonal Violence, 12*(3), 392–406. doi: 10.1177/088626097012003005

Cameron, P., & Biber, H. (1973). Sexual thought throughout the life-span. *Gerontologist, 13*(2), 144–147. doi:10.1093/geront/13.2.144

Carnes, P. J. (1998). The case for sexual anorexia: An interim report on 144 patients with sexual disorders. *Sexual Addiction and Compulsivity, 5*(4), 293–309. doi:10.1080/10720169808402338

Carroll, L. (2016, April 22). Dolphins are rapists, "Unbreakable Kimmy Schmidt" claims wrongly. *PolitiFact.* Retrieved from http://www.politifact.com/punditfact/statements/2016/apr/22/unbreakable-kimmy-schmidt/dolphins-rapists-unbreakable-kimmy-schmidt

Carvalho, J., Quinta-Gomes, A., & Nobre, P. J. (2013). The sexual functioning profile of a nonforensic sample of individuals reporting sexual aggression against women. *Journal of Sexual Medicine, 10*(7), 1744–1754. doi: 10.1111/jsm.12188

Cassidy, L., & Hurell, R. M. (1995). The influence of victim's attire on adolescents' judgments of date rape. *Adolescence, 30*(118), 319–323.

Castano, E. (2004). In case of death, cling to the ingroup. *European Journal of Social Psychology, 34*, 375–384. doi:10.1002/ejsp.211

Cavazos-Rehg, P. A., Krauss, M. J., Spitznagel, E. L., Schootman, M., Bucholz, K. K., Peipert, J. F., ... Bierut, L. J. (2009). Age of sexual debut among US adolescents. *Contraception, 80*(2), 158–162. doi:10.1016/

j.contraception.2009.02.014

Chasin, C. D. (2011). Theoretical issues in the study of asexuality. *Archives of Sexual Behavior, 40*(4), 713–723. doi:10.1007/s10508-011-9757-x

Childs, M. (1980). Chigo monogatari: Love stories or Buddhist sermons? *Monumenta Nipponica, 35*, 127–151.

Chivers, M. L., Seto, M. C., Lalumière, M. L., Laan, E., & Grimbos, T. (2010). Agreement of self-reported and genital measures of sexual arousal in men and women: A meta-analysis. *Archives of Sexual Behavior, 39*(1), 5–56. doi:10.1007/s10508-009-9556-9

Christopher, F. S., Owens, L. A., & Stecker, H. L. (1993). An examination of single men's and women's sexual aggressiveness in dating relationships. *Journal of Social and Personal Relationships, 10*(4), 511–527. doi:10.1177/0265407593104003

Clifford, R. (1978). Development of masturbation in college women. *Archives of Sexual Behavior, 7*(6), 559–573. doi:10.1007/BF01541922

Coelho, G. A., Rodrigues, E., Andersen, M. L., Tufik, S., & Hachul, H. (2013). Psychotherapy improved the sleep quality in a patient who was a victim of child sexual abuse: A case report. *Journal of Sexual Medicine, 10*(12), 3146–3150. doi:10.1111/jsm.12323

Committee on Lesbian and Gay Concerns, American Psychological Association. (1991). Avoiding heterosexual bias in language. *American Psychologist, 46*(9), 973–974. doi:10.1037/0003-066X.46.9.973

Cortoni, F., Hanson, R. K., & Coache, M.-È. (2010). The recidivism rates of female sexual offenders are low: A meta-analysis. *Sexual Abuse, 22*(4), 387–401. doi:10.1177/1079063210372142

Cowan, G. (2009). The causes of rape: Antisociality and reproductive strategies. *Sex Roles, 61*(1, 2), 136–139. doi:10.1007/s11199-009-9592-x

Cox, G. (1995). De virginibus puerisque: The function of the human foreskin considered from an evolutionary perspective. *Medical Hypotheses, 45*(6), 617–621. doi:10.1016/0306-9877(95)90248-1

Crews, D., Grassman, M., & Lindzey, J. (1986). Behavioral facilitation of reproduction in sexual and unisexual whiptail lizards. *Proceedings of the National Academy of Sciences, 83*(24), 9547–9550. doi:10.1073/pnas.83.24.9547

Daleiden, E. L., Kaufman, K. L., Hilliker, D. R., & O'Neil, J. N. (1998). The sexual histories and fantasies of youthful males: A comparison of sexual offending, nonsexual offending, and nonoffending groups. *Sexual Abuse, 10*(3), 195–209. doi:10.1023/A:1021365804076

Dansky, B. S., Brewerton, T. D., Kilpatrick, D. G., & O'Neil, P. M. (1997). The National Women's Study: Relationship of victimization and posttraumatic stress disorder to bulimia nervosa. *International Journal of Eating Disorders, 21*(3), 213–228. doi:10.1002/(SICI)1098-108X(199704)21:3<213::AID-EAT2>3.0.CO;2-N

Davidson, J. K. (1984). Autoeroticism, sexual satisfaction, and sexual adjustment among university females: Past and current patterns. *Deviant Behavior, 5*(1, 4), 121–140. doi:10.1080/01639625.1984.9967637

Davis, D. L., & Whitten, R. G. (1987). The cross-cultural study of human sexuality. *Annual Review of Anthropology, 16*(1), 69–98. doi:10.1146/annurev.an.16.100187.000441 de Silva, W. P. (1999). ABC of sexual health: Sexual variations. *BMJ, 318*(7184), 654–656. doi:10.1136/bmj.318.7184.654

Dean, K. E., & Malamuth, N. M. (1997). Characteristics of men who aggress sexually and of men who imagine aggressing: Risk and moderating variables. *Journal of Personality and Social Psychology, 72*(2), 449–455. doi:10.1037/0022-3514.72.2.449

DeForest, C. E. (2011, March 24). *drzowie comments on ELI5: Why do we wear clothes/Are ashamed to be naked?* Retrieved from https://www.reddit.com/r/explainlikeimfive/comments/rbosq/x/c44ihs6

DeJong, W. (1999). Rape and physical attractiveness: Judgments concerning the likelihood of victimization. *Psychological Reports, 85*(1), 32–34. doi:10.2466/PR0.85.5.32-34

Ditto, P. H., Pizarro, D. A., Epstein, E. B., Jacobson, J. A., & MacDonald, T. K. (2006). Visceral influences on risk-taking behavior. *Journal of Behavioral Decision Making, 19*, 99–113. doi:10.1002/bdm.520

Donovan, B. (2000). The repertoire of human efforts to avoid sexually transmissible diseases: past and present. Part 2: Strategies used during or after sex. *Sexually Transmitted Infections, 76*(2), 88–93. doi:10.1136/sti.76.2.88

Drach, K. M., Wientzen, J., & Ricci, L. R. (2001). The diagnostic utility of sexual behavior problems in diagnosing sexual abuse in a forensic child abuse evaluation clinic. *Child Abuse and Neglect, 25*(4), 489–503. doi:10.1016/S0145-2134(01)00222-8

Dreber, A., Gerdes, C., & Gränsmark, P. (2013). Beauty queens and battling knights: Risk taking and attractiveness in chess. *Journal of Economic Behavior and Organization, 90*, 1–18. doi:10.1016/j.jebo.2013.03.006

Dutton, D. G., & Aron, A. P. (1974). Some evidence for heightened sexual attraction under conditions of high anxiety. *Journal of Personality and Social Psychology, 30*, 510–517. doi:10.1037/h0037031

Ebel-Lam, A. P., MacDonald, T. K., Zanna, M. P., & Fong, G. T. (2009). An experimental investigation of the interactive effects of alcohol and sexual arousal on intentions to have unprotected sex. *Basic and Applied Social Psychology, 31*(3), 226–233. doi:10.1080/01973530903058383

Echols, A. (1989). *Daring to be bad: Radical feminism in America, 1967-1975.* Minneapolis, MN: University of Minnesota Press. ISBN 978-0-8166-1786-9.

Ekmekçioğlu, O., Inci, M., Demirci, D., & Tatlişen, A. (2005). Effects of sildenafil citrate on ejaculation latency, detumescence time, and refractory period: Placebo-controlled, double-blind, crossover laboratory setting study. *Urology, 65*(2), 347–352. doi:10.1016/j.urology.2004.09.012

Epstude, K., & Förster, J. (2011). Seeing love, or seeing lust: How people interpret ambiguous romantic situations. *Journal of Experimental Social Psychology, 47*(5), 1017–1020. doi:10.1016/j.jesp.2011.03.019

Evans-Pritchard, E. E. (1970). Sexual inversion among the Azande. *American Anthropologist, 72*(6), 1428–1434. doi:10.1525/aa.1970.72.6.02a00170

Feinstein, B. A., Humphreys, K. L., Bovin, M. J., Marx, B. P., & Resick, P. A. (2011). Victim–offender relationship status moderates the relationships of peritraumatic emotional responses, active resistance, and posttraumatic stress symptomatology in female rape survivors. *Psychological Trauma, 3*(2), 192–200. doi:10.1037/a0021652

Felson, R. B., & Cundiff, P. R. (2012). Age and sexual assault during robberies. *Evolution and Human Behavior, 33*(1), 10–16. doi:10.1016/j.evolhumbehav.2011.04.002

Felson, R. B., & Krohn, M. (1990). Motives for rape. *Journal of Research in Crime and Delinquency, 27,* 222–242. doi:10.1177/0022427890027003002

Fessler, D. M. T., & Navarrete, C. D. (2003). Domain-specific variation in disgust sensitivity across the menstrual cycle. *Evolution and Human Behavior, 24*(6), 406–417. doi:10.1016/S1090-5138(03)00054-0

Finkelhor, D., Hammer, H., & Sedlak, A. J. (2008). *Sexually assaulted children: National estimates and characteristics.* Washington, DC: Office of Juvenile Justice and Delinquency Prevention. Retrieved from https://www.ncjrs.gov/pdffiles1/ojjdp/214383.pdf

Fisher, W. A., White, L. A., Byrne, D., & Kelley, K. (1988). Erotophobia-erotophilia as a dimension of personality. *Journal of Sex Research, 25*(1), 123–151. doi:10.1080/00224498809551448

Fitzgerald, L. F., Drasgow, F., Hulin, C. L., Gelfand, M. J., & Magley, V. J. (1997). Antecedents and consequences of sexual harassment in organizations: A test of an integrated model. *Journal of Applied Psychology, 82*(4), 578–589. doi:10.1037/0021-9010.82.4.578. Retrieved from http://www.gelfand.umd.edu/Fitzgeraldetal1997.pdf

Fitzgerald, L. F., Gelfand, M. J., & Drasgow, F. (1995). Measuring sexual harassment: Theoretical and psychometric advances. *Basic and Applied Social Psychology, 17*(4), 425–445. doi:10.1207/s15324834basp1704_2

Flowe, H. D., Stewart, J., Sleath, E. R., & Palmer, F. T. (2011). Public house patrons' engagement in hypothetical sexual assault: A test of Alcohol Myopia Theory in a field setting. *Aggressive Behavior, 37*(6), 547–558. doi:10.1002/ab.20410

Francoeur, R. T., & Noonan, R. J. (Eds.). (2004). *The Continuum complete international encyclopedia of sexuality.* New York, NY: Continuum. Retrieved from https://kinseyinstitute.org/collections/archival/ccies.php

Frankenhuis, W. E., & Karremans, J. C. (2012). Uncommitted men match their risk taking to female preferences, while committed men do the opposite. *Journal of Experimental Social Psychology, 48*(1), 428–431. doi:10.1016/j.jesp.2011.09.001

Frankenhuis, W. E., Dostsch, R., Karremans, J. C., & Wigboldus, D. H. J. (2010). Male physical risk taking in a virtual environment. *Journal of Evolutionary Psychology, 8*(1), 75–86. doi:10.1556/JEP.8.2010.1.6

Freund, K., & Blanchard, R. (1989). Phallometric diagnosis of pedophilia. *Journal of Consulting and Clinical Psychology, 57*(1), 100–105. doi:10.1037/0022-006X.57.1.100

Fry, D. P. (1998). Anthropological perspectives on aggression: Sex differences and cultural variation. *Aggressive Behavior, 24*(2), 81–95. doi:10.1002/(SICI)1098-2337(1998)24:2<81::AID-AB1>3.0.CO;2-V

Förster, J. (2010). How love and sex can influence recognition of faces and words: A processing model account. *European Journal of Social Psychology, 40*(3), 524–535.

Förster, J., Özelsel, A., & Epstude, K. (2010). How love and lust change people's perception of relationship partners. *Journal of Experimental Social Psychology, 46*(2), 237–246. doi:10.1016/j.jesp.2009.08.009

Gagnon, J. H., & Simon, W. (1968). The social meaning of prison homosexuality. *Federal Probation, 32*, 23–29.

Galdikas, B. M. F. (1995). *Reflections of Eden: My years with the orangutans of Borneo*. Boston, MA: Little, Brown. ISBN 978-0-316-30181-7.

Garrison, E. G., & Kobor, P. C. (2002). Weathering a political storm: A contextual perspective on a psychological research controversy. *American Psychologist, 57*(3), 165–175. doi:10.1037/0003-066X.57.3.165

Girelli, S. A., Resick, P. A., Marhoefer-Dvorak, S., & Hutter, C. K. (1986). Subjective distress and violence during rape: Their effects on long-term fear. *Violence and Victims, 1*(1), 35–46.

Glassgold, J. M., Beckstead, L., Drescher, J., Greene, B., Miller, R. L., & Worthington, R. L. (2009). *Report of the task force on appropriate therapeutic responses to sexual orientation*. Washington, DC: American Psychological Association. Retrieved from http://www.apa.org/pi/lgbt/resources/therapeutic-response.pdf

Godin, J. G., & Dugatkin, L. A. (1996). Female mating preference for bold males in the guppy, *Poecilia reticulata*. *Proceedings of the National Academy of Sciences, 93*(19), 10262–10267. doi:10.1073/pnas.93.19.10262

Goetz, C. D., Easton, J. A., Lewis, D. M. G., & Buss, D. M. (2012). Sexual exploitability: Observable cues and their link to sexual attraction. *Evolution and Human Behavior, 33*(4), 417–426. doi:10.1016/j.evolhumbehav.2011.12.004

Goldenberg, J. L., Cox, C. R., Pyszczynski, T., Greenberg, J., & Solomon, S. (2002). Understanding human ambivalence about sex: The effects of stripping sex of meaning. *Journal of Sex Research, 39*(4), 310–320. doi:10.1080/00224490209552155

Goldenberg, J. L., Hart, J., Pyszczynski, T., Warnica, G. M., Landau, M., & Thomas, L. (2006). Ambivalence toward the body: Death, neuroticism, and the flight from physical sensation. *Personality and Social Psychology Bulletin, 32*(9), 1264–1277. doi:10.1177/0146167206289505

Goldenberg, J. L., McCoy, S. K., Pyszczynski, T., Greenberg, J., & Solomon, S. (2000). The body as a source of self-esteem: The effect of mortality salience on identification with one's body, interest in sex, and appearance monitoring. *Journal of Personality and Social Psychology, 79*(1), 118–130. doi:10.1037/0022-3514.79.1.118

Goldenberg, J. L., Pyszczynski, T., McCoy, S. K., Greenberg, J., & Solomon, S. (1999). Death, sex, love, and neuroticism: Why is sex such a problem? *Journal of Personality and Social Psychology, 77*(6), 1173–1187. doi:10.1037/0022-3514.77.6.1173

Greenberg, J. S. (1972). The masturbatory behavior of college students. *Psychology in the Schools, 9*(4), 427–432. `doi: 10.1002/1520-6807(197210)9:4<427::AID-PITS2310090417>3.0.CO;2-Z`

Greenberg, J., Pyszczynski, T., Solomon, S., Rosenblatt, A., Veeder, M., Kirkland, S., & Lyon, D. (1990). Evidence for terror management theory II: The effects of mortality salience on reactions to those who threaten or bolster the cultural worldview. *Journal of Personality and Social Psychology, 58*(2), 308–318. `doi:10.1037/0022-3514.58.2.308`

Greenberg, J., Schimel, J., Martens, A., Solomon, S., & Pyszcznyski, T. (2001). Sympathy for the devil: Evidence that reminding Whites of their mortality promotes more favorable reactions to White racists. *Motivation and Emotion, 25*, 113–133. `doi:10.1023/A:1010613909207`

Greenberg, J., Solomon, S., & Arndt, J. (2008). A basic but uniquely human motivation: Terror management theory. In J. Y. Shah & W. L. Gardner (Eds.), *Handbook of motivation science* (pp. 114–134). New York, NY: The Guilford Press.

Greene, D. M., & Navarro, R. L. (1998). Situation-specific assertiveness in the epidemiology of sexual victimization among university women. *Psychology of Women Quarterly, 22*(4), 589–604. `doi:10.1111/j.1471-6402.1998.tb00179.x`

Gregg, A. (1948). Preface. In A. C. Kinsey, W. B. Pomeroy, & C. E. Martin (Eds.), *Sexual behavior in the human male*. Philadelphia, PA: Saunders.

Griffin, M. G., Resick, P. A., & Mechanic, M. B. (1997). Objective assessment of peritraumatic dissociation: Psychophysiological indicators. *American Journal of Psychiatry, 154*(8), 1081–1088.

Grindal, S. D., Collard, T. S., Brigham, R. M., & Barclay, R. M. R. (1992). The influence of precipitation on reproduction by *Myotis* bats in British Columbia. *American Midland Naturalist, 128*(2), 339–344. Retrieved from `http://www.jstor.org.proxy.library.stonybrook.edu/stable/2426468`

Griskevicius, V., Tybur, J. M., Gangestad, S. W., Perea, E. F., Shapiro, J. R., & Kenrick, D. T. (2009). Aggress to impress: Hostility as an evolved context-dependent strategy. *Journal of Personality and Social Psychology, 96*(5), 980–994. `doi:10.1037/a0013907`

Gutner, C. A., Rizvi, S. L., Monson, C. M., & Resick, P. A. (2006). Changes in coping strategies, relationship to the perpetrator, and posttraumatic distress in female crime victims. *Journal of Traumatic Stress, 19*(6), 813–823. `doi:10.1002/jts.20158`

Guéguen, N. (2011). The effect of women's suggestive clothing on men's behavior and judgement: A field study. *Psychological Reports, 109*(2), 635–638. `doi:10.2466/07.17.PR0.109.5.635-638`

Haack, S. (2001). After my own heart: Dorothy L. Sayers's feminism. *New Criterion, 19*(9), 10–14. Retrieved from `http://www.newcriterion.com/articles.cfm/sayers-haack-2180`

Haidt, J., Bjorklund, F., & Murphy, S. (2000). *Moral dumbfounding: When intuition finds no reason*. Retrieved from `http://faculty.virginia.edu/haidtlab/articles/manuscripts/haidt.bjorklund.working-`

`paper.when%20intuition%20finds%20no%20reason.pub603.doc`

Hall, G. C. N., Hirschman, R., & Oliver, L. L. (1995). Sexual arousal and arousability to pedophilic stimuli in a community sample of normal men. *Behavior Therapy, 26*(4), 681–694. `doi:10.1016/S0005-7894(05)80039-5`

Hall, G. C. N., Shondrick, D. D., & Hirschman, R. (1993). The role of sexual arousal in sexually aggressive behavior: A meta-analysis. *Journal of Consulting and Clinical Psychology, 61*(6), 1091–1095. `doi:10.1037/0022-006X.61.6.1091`

Harris, G. T., Lalumière, M. L., Seto, M. C., Rice, M. E., & Chaplin, T. C. (2012). Explaining the erectile responses of rapists to rape stories: The contributions of sexual activity, non-consent, and violence with injury. *Archives of Sexual Behavior, 41*(1), 221–229. `doi:10.1007/s10508-012-9940-8`

Heilbrun, A. B., Jr., & Loftus, M. P. (1986). The role of sadism and peer pressure in the sexual aggression of male college students. *Journal of Sex Research, 22*(3), 320–332. `doi:10.1080/00224498609551312`

Herbenick, D., Reece, M., Schick, V., Sanders, S. A., Dodge, B., & Fortenberry, J. D. (2010). Sexual behavior in the United States: Results from a national probability sample of men and women ages 14-94. *Journal of Sexual Medicine, 7*(Suppl. 5), 255–265. `doi:10.1111/j.1743-6109.2010.02012.x`

Hewlett, B. S., & Hewlett, B. L. (2010). Sex and searching for children among Aka foragers and Ngandu farmers of central Africa. *African Study Monographs, 31*(3), 107–125. `doi:10.14989/128939`

Hickson, F. C. I., Davies, P. M., Hunt, A. J., Weatherburn, P., McManus, T. J., & Coxon, A. P. M. (1994). Gay men as victims of nonconsensual sex. *Archives of Sexual Behavior, 23*(3), 281–294. `doi:10.1007/BF01541564`

Hines, D. A., & Finkelhor, D. (2007). Statutory sex crime relationships between juveniles and adults: A review of social scientific research. *Aggression and Violent Behavior, 12*(3), 300–314. `doi:10.1016/j.avb.2006.10.001`

Hoffmann, H. (2012). Considering the role of conditioning in sexual orientation. *Archives of Sexual Behavior, 41*(1), 63–71. `doi:10.1007/s10508-012-9915-9`

Hohmann, G., & Fruth, B. (2000). Use and function of genital contacts among female bonobos. *Animal Behaviour, 60*(1), 107–120. `doi:10.1006/anbe.2000.1451`

Hunter, F. M., & Davis, L. S. (1998). Female Adélie Penguins acquire nest material from extrapair males after engaging in extrapair copulations. *The Auk, 115*(2), 526–528. Retrieved from `http://elibrary.unm.edu/sora/Auk/v115n02/p0526-p0528.pdf`

Hunter, J. (2008). The political use and abuse of the "pedophile". *Journal of Homosexuality, 55*(3), 350–387. `doi:10.1080/00918360802345073`

Idani, G. (1991). Social relationships between immigrant and resident bonobo (*Pan paniscus*) females at Wamba. *Folia Primatologica, 57*(2), 83–95. `doi:10.1159/000156568`

Ipeirotis, P. G. (2010). *Demographics of Mechanical Turk* (Technical Report No. CeDER-10-01). New York, NY: New York University. Retrieved from http://hdl.handle.net/2451/29585

Jiang, Y., Costello, P., Fang, F., Huang, M., He, S., & Purves, D. (2006). A gender- and sexual orientation-dependent spatial attentional effect of invisible images. *Proceedings of the National Academy of Sciences, 103*(45), 17048–17052. doi:10.1073/pnas.0605678103

Jones, J. H. (1997). *Alfred C. Kinsey: A public/private life.* New York, NY: W. W. Norton. ISBN 978-0-393-04086-9.

Jones, J. S., Rossman, L., Wynn, B. N., & Ostovar, H. (2010). Assailants' sexual dysfunction during rape: Prevalence and relationship to genital trauma in female victims. *Journal of Emergency Medicine, 38*(4), 529–535. doi:10.1016/j.jemermed.2008.09.037

Kanekar, S., & Kolsawalla, M. B. (1980). Responsibility of a rape victim in relation to her respectability, attractiveness, and provocativeness. *Journal of Social Psychology, 112*(1), 153–154. doi:10.1080/00224545.1980.9924310

Kano, T. (1980). Social behavior of wild pygmy chimpanzees (*Pan paniscus*) of Wamba: A preliminary report. *Journal of Human Evolution, 9*(4), 243–260. doi:10.1016/0047-2484(80)90053-6

Karremans, J. C., Stroebe, W., & Claus, J. (2006). Beyond Vicary's fantasies: The impact of subliminal priming and brand choice. *Journal of Experimental Social Psychology, 42*, 792–798. doi:10.1016/j.jesp.2005.12.002

Karremans, J. C., Verwijmeren, T., Pronk, T. M., & Reitsma, M. (2009). Interacting with women can impair men's cognitive functioning. *Journal of Experimental Social Psychology, 45*(4), 1041–1044. doi:10.1016/j.jesp.2009.05.004

Kavaliers, M., Choleris, E., & Colwell, D. D. (2001). Brief exposure to female odors "emboldens" male mice by reducing predator-induced behavioral and hormonal responses. *Hormones and Behavior, 40*(4), 497–509. doi:10.1006/hbeh.2001.1714

Kavaliers, M., Devidze, N., Choleris, E., Fudge, M., Gustafsson, J. A., Korach, K. S., ... Ogawa, S. (2008). Estrogen receptors alpha and beta mediate different aspects of the facilitatory effects of female cues on male risk taking. *Psychoneuroendocrinology, 33*(5), 634–642. doi:10.1016/j.psyneuen.2008.02.003

Kavanagh, D. J., Andrade, J., & May, J. (2005). Imaginary relish and exquisite torture: The elaborated intrusion theory of desire. *Psychological Review, 112*(2), 446–467. doi:10.1037/0033-295X.112.2.446

Kennair, L. E. O., & Bendixen, M. (2012). Sociosexuality as predictor of sexual harassment and coercion in female and male high school students. *Evolution and Human Behavior, 33*(5), 479–490. doi:10.1016/j.evolhumbehav.2012.01.001

Kilpatrick, D. G., Saunders, B. E., Amick-McMullan, A., Best, C. L., Veronen, L. J., & Resnick, H. S. (1989). Victim and crime factors associated with the development of crime-related post-traumatic stress disorder. *Behavior Therapy, 20*(2), 199–214. doi:10.1016/S0005-7894(89)80069-3

Kim, B. K., & Zauberman, G. (2013). Can Victoria's Secret change the future? A subjective time perception account of sexual-cue effects on impatience. *Journal of Experimental Psychology: General, 142*(2), 328–335. doi:

`10.1037/a0028954`

Kimball, G. (1993). Aztec homosexuality: The textual evidence. *Journal of Homosexuality, 26*, 7–24. `doi:10.1300/J082v26n01_02`

Kinsey, A. C., Pomeroy, W. B., & Martin, C. E. (1948). *Sexual behavior in the human male*. Philadelphia, PA: Saunders.

Kinsey, A. C., Pomeroy, W. B., Martin, C. E., & Gebhard, P. H. (1953). *Sexual behavior in the human female*. Philadelphia, PA: Saunders.

Knutson, B., Wimmer, G. E., Kuhnen, C. M., & Winkielman, P. (2008). Nucleus accumbens activation mediates the influence of reward cues on financial risk taking. *NeuroReport, 19*(5), 509–513. `doi:10.1097/WNR.0b013e3282f85c01`

Koedt, A. (1970). *The myth of the vaginal orgasm*. Retrieved from `http://www.cwluherstory.org/myth-of-the-vaginal-orgasm.html`

Komisaruk, B. R., Gerdes, C. A., & Whipple, B. (1997). "Complete" spinal cord injury does not block perceptual responses to genital self-stimulation in women. *Archives of Neurology, 54*(12), 1513–1520. `doi:10.1001/archneur.1997.00550240063014`

Kontula, O., & Haavio-Mannila, E. (2002). Masturbation in a generational perspective. *Journal of Psychology and Human Sexuality, 14*(2, 3), 49–83. `doi:10.1300/J056v14n02_05`

Koppel, H. (1987). *Lifetime likelihood of victimization*. Washington, DC: US Department of Justice, Bureau of Justice Statistics. Retrieved from `http://www.bjs.gov/content/pub/pdf/llv.pdf`

Krahé, B., Waizenhöfer, E., & Möller, I. (2003). Women's sexual aggression against men: Prevalence and predictors. *Sex Roles, 49*(5, 6), 219–232. `doi:10.1023/A:1024648106477`

Lacasse, A., & Mendelson, M. J. (2007). Sexual coercion among adolescents: Victims and perpetrators. *Journal of Interpersonal Violence, 22*(4), 424–437. `doi:10.1177/0886260506297027`

Laier, C., Schulte, F. P., & Brand, M. (2013). Pornographic picture processing interferes with working memory performance. *Journal of Sex Research, 50*(7), 642–652. `doi:10.1080/00224499.2012.716873`

Lalumière, M. L., & Quinsey, V. L. (1994). The discriminability of rapists from non-sex offenders using phallometric measures: A meta-analysis. *Criminal Justice and Behavior, 21*(1), 150–175. `doi:10.1177/0093854894021001010`. Retrieved from `http://web.archive.org/web/20160322050110/http://www.queensu.ca/psychology/sites/webpublish.queensu.ca.psycwww/files/files/Faculty/Vern%20Qunisey/LalumiereQuinseyrapis20metaCJB1994.pdf`

Lalumière, M. L., & Quinsey, V. L. (1996). Sexual deviance, antisociality, mating effort, and the use of sexually coercive behaviors. *Personality and Individual Differences, 21*(1), 33–48. `doi:10.1016/0191-8869(96)00059-1`

Lalumière, M. L., Chalmers, L. J., Quinsey, V. L., & Seto, M. C. (1996). A test of the mate deprivation hypothesis of sexual coercion. *Ethology and Sociobiology, 17*(5), 299–318. `doi:10.1016/S0162-3095(96)00076-3`

Lalumière, M. L., Harris, G. T., Quinsey, V. L., & Rice, M. E. (2005a).

Antisociality and mating effort. In *The causes of rape: Understanding individual differences in male propensity for sexual aggression.* Washington, DC: American Psychological Association. ISBN 978-1-59147-186-8.

Lalumière, M. L., Harris, G. T., Quinsey, V. L., & Rice, M. E. (2005b). Forced copulation in the animal kingdom. In *The causes of rape: Understanding individual differences in male propensity for sexual aggression.* Washington, DC: American Psychological Association. ISBN 978-1-59147-186-8.

Lalumière, M. L., Quinsey, V. L., Harris, G. T., Rice, M. E., & Trautrimas, C. (2003). Are rapists differentially aroused by coercive sex in phallometric assessments? *Annals of the New York Academy of Sciences, 989*, 211–224. doi:10.1111/j.1749-6632.2003.tb07307.x

Landry, C. E., Lange, A., List, J. A., Price, M. K., & Rupp, N. G. (2006). Toward an understanding of the economics of charity: Evidence from a field experiment. *Quarterly Journal of Economics, 121*(2), 747–782. doi:10.1162/qjec.2006.121.2.747

Larsson, I. (2000). *Child sexuality and sexual behavior* (Article No. 2001-123-20). Swedish National Board of Health and Welfare. Retrieved from http://www.jeanyveshayez.net/tele-pdf/larsson.pdf

Laumann, E. O., Gagnon, J., Michael, R. T., & Michaels, S. (1994). *The social organization of sexuality: Sexual practices in the United States.* Chicago, IL: University of Chicago Press.

Levan, K. E., Fedina, T. Y., & Lewis, S. M. (2009). Testing multiple hypotheses for the maintenance of male homosexual copulatory behaviour in flour beetles. *Journal of Evolutionary Biology, 22*(1), 60–70. doi:10.1111/j.1420-9101.2008.01616.x

Levin, R. J. (2009). Revisiting post-ejaculation refractory time—What we know and what we do not know in males and in females. *Journal of Sexual Medicine, 6*(9), 2376–2389. doi:10.1111/j.1743-6109.2009.01350.x

Levin, R. J., & van Berlo, W. (2004). Sexual arousal and orgasm in subjects who experience forced or non-consensual sexual stimulation—a review. *Journal of Clinical Forensic Medicine, 11*(2), 82–88. doi:10.1016/j.jcfm.2003.10.008

Li, J., Yin, H., & Zhou, L. (2007). Non-reproductive copulation behavior among Tibetan macaques (*Macaca thibetana*) at Huangshan, China. *Primates, 48*(1), 64–72. doi:10.1007/s10329-006-0002-5

Lloyd, E. A. (2006). *The case of the female orgasm: Bias in the science of evolution.* Cambridge, MA: Harvard University Press. ISBN 0674022467.

Loewenstein, G. (2009, May 21). *George Loewenstein on Like, Want, and Sex, by gender & age* [Video file]. National Institute on Aging. Retrieved from http://www.youtube.com/watch?v=P97yCvUHyNA

Loewenstein, G., Nagin, D., & Paternoster, R. (1997). The effect of sexual arousal on expectations of sexual forcefulness. *Journal of Research in Crime and Delinquency, 34*(4), 443–473. doi:10.1177/0022427897034004003

Lohr, B. A., Adams, H. E., & Davis, J. M. (1997). Sexual arousal to erotic and aggressive stimuli in sexually coercive and noncoercive men. *Journal of*

Abnormal Psychology, 106(2), 230–242. doi:10.1037/0021-843X. 106.2.230

Lonsway, K. A., & Fitzgerald, L. F. (1994). Rape myths: In review. *Psychology of Women Quarterly, 18*(2), 133–164. doi:10.1111/j. 1471-6402.1994.tb00448.x

Luhmann, C. C., Ishida, K., & Hajcak, G. (2011). Intolerance of uncertainty and decisions about delayed, probabilistic rewards. *Behavior Therapy, 42*, 378–386. doi:10.1016/j.beth.2010.09.002. Retrieved from http://www.psychology.stonybrook.edu/cluhmann-/papers/luhmann-2011-bt.pdf

Maisto, S. A., Palfai, T., Vanable, P. A., Heath, J., & Woolf-King, S. E. (2012). The effects of alcohol and sexual arousal on determinants of sexual risk in men who have sex with men. *Archives of Sexual Behavior, 41*(4), 971–986. doi:10.1007/s10508-011-9846-x

Malamuth, N. M. (1986). Predictors of naturalistic sexual aggression. *Journal of Personality and Social Psychology, 50*, 953–962. doi:10.1037/0022-3514.50.5.953

Manson, J. H., Perry, S., & Parish, A. R. (1997). Nonconceptive sexual behavior in bonobos and capuchins. *International Journal of Primatology, 18*(5), 767–786. doi:10.1023/A:1026395829818

Martin, E. K., Taft, C. T., & Resick, P. A. (2007). A review of marital rape. *Aggression and Violent Behavior, 12*(3), 329–347. doi:10.1016/j.avb.2006.10.003

McCallum, N. L., & McGlone, M. S. (2011). Death be not profane: Mortality salience and euphemism use. *Western Journal of Communication, 75*(5), 565–584. doi:10.1080/10570314.2011.608405

McClintock, M. K., & Herdt, G. (1996). Rethinking puberty: The development of sexual attraction. *Current Directions in Psychological Science, 5*(6), 178–183. doi:10.1111/1467-8721.ep11512422

Mock, S. E., & Eibach, R. P. (2012). Stability and change in sexual orientation identity over a 10-year period in adulthood. *Archives of Sexual Behavior, 41*(3), 641–648. doi:10.1007/s10508-011-9761-1

Mondaini, N., Ponchietti, R., Muir, G. H., Montorsi, F., Di Loro, F., Lombardi, G., & Rizzo, M. (2003). Sildenafil does not improve sexual function in men without erectile dysfunction but does reduce the postorgasmic refractory time. *International Journal of Impotence Research, 15*(3), 225–228. doi:10.1038/sj.ijir.3901005

Moor, A., & Farchi, M. (2011). Is rape-related self blame distinct from other post traumatic attributions of blame? A comparison of severity and implications for treatment. *Women and Therapy, 34*(4), 447–460. doi:10.1080/02703149.2011.591671

Muehlenhard, C. L., & Peterson, Z. D. (2005). Wanting and not wanting sex: The missing discourse of ambivalence. *Feminism and Psychology, 15*(1), 15–20. doi:10.1177/0959353505049698

Mussweiler, T., & Förster, J. (2000). The sex → aggression link: A perception-behavior dissociation. *Journal of Personality and Social Psychology, 79*(4), 507–520. doi:10.1037/0022-3514.79.4.507

Nauts, S., Metzmacher, M., Verwijmeren, T., Rommeswinkel, V., & Karremans, J. C. (2012). The mere anticipation of an interaction with a woman can impair men's cognitive performance. *Archives of Sexual Behavior, 41*(4), 1051–1056. doi:10.1007/s10508-011-9860-z

Nisbett, R. E., & Wilson, T. D. (1977). Telling more than we can know: Verbal reports on mental processes. *Psychological Review, 84,* 231–259. doi: 10.1037/0033-295X.84.3.231

Nordgren, L. F., van Harreveld, F., & van der Pligt, J. (2009). The restraint bias: How the illusion of self-restraint promotes impulsive behavior. *Psychological Science, 20*(12), 1523–1528. doi:10.1111/j. 1467-9280.2009.02468.x

North, R. (2011, July 4). if you chose seventeen between panels one and two, congratulations, but ask yourself this: why do you respond to "dromiceiomimus"? *Dinosaur Comics.* Retrieved from http:// qwantz.com?comic=1993

Okami, P., Olmstead, R., & Abramson, P. R. (1997). Sexual experiences in early childhood: 18-year longitudinal data from the UCLA Family Lifestyles Project. *Journal of Sex Research, 34*(4), 339–347. doi: 10.1080/00224499709551902

Ott, M. Q., Corliss, H. L., Wypij, D., Rosario, M., & Austin, S. B. (2011). Stability and change in self-reported sexual orientation identity in young people: Application of mobility metrics. *Archives of Sexual Behavior, 40*(3), 519–532. doi:10.1007/s10508-010-9691-3

Palmer, C. T. (1988). Twelve reasons why rape is not sexually motivated: A skeptical examination. *Journal of Sex Research, 25*(4), 512–530. doi: 10.1080/00224498809551479

Palmer, C. T. (1989). Is rape a cultural universal? A re-examination of the ethnographic data. *Ethnology, 28*(1), 1–16. Retrieved from http:// www.jstor.org/stable/3773639

Pari, A. G. (2013, February 23). *IAMA sexual assault therapist discussing when orgasm happens during rape. AMA! : IAmA.* Retrieved from https:// www.reddit.com/r/IAmA/comments/193e3x

Peeters, C. F. W., Klaassen, C. A. J., & van de Wiel, M. A. (2015). *Evaluating the scientific veracity of publications by Dr. Jens Förster.* Retrieved from http://www.uva.nl/binaries/content/assets/uva/nl/ persvoorlichting/uva-nieuws/jfcase_fullreport.pdf

Percy, W. A., III. (2005). Reconsiderations about Greek homosexualities. *Journal of Homosexuality, 49*(3, 4), 13–61. doi:10.1300/ J082v49n03_02

Petersen, J. L., & Hyde, J. S. (2009). A longitudinal investigation of peer sexual harassment victimization in adolescence. *Journal of Adolescence, 32*(5), 1173–1188. doi:10.1016/j.adolescence.2009.01.011

Petersen, J. L., & Hyde, J. S. (2013). Peer sexual harassment and disordered eating in early adolescence. *Developmental Psychology, 49*(1), 184–195. doi:10.1037/a0028247

Peterson, Z. D., Janssen, E., & Heiman, J. R. (2010). The association between sexual aggression and HIV risk behavior in heterosexual men. *Journal of Interpersonal Violence, 25*(3), 538–556. doi: 10.1177/0886260509334414

Pinkerton, S. D., Bogart, L. M., Cecil, H., & Abramson, P. R. (2002). Factors associated with masturbation in collegiate sample. *Journal of Psychology and Human Sexuality, 14*(2, 3), 103–121. doi:10.1300/ J056v14n02_07

Ponseti, J., Granert, O., Jansen, O., Wolff, S., Mehdorn, H., Bosinski, H., & Siebner, H. (2009). Assessment of sexual orientation using the hemodynamic brain response to visual sexual stimuli. *Journal of Sexual Medicine, 6*(6), 1628–1634. doi:10.1111/j. 1743-6109.2009.01233.x

Powdermaker, H. (1933). *Life in Lesu.* New York, NY: Norton.

Pratkanis, A. R. (1992). The cargo-cult science of subliminal persuasion. *Skeptical Inquirer, 16.* Retrieved from http://www.csicop.org/si/ show/cargo-cult_science_of_subliminal_persuasion

Quinsey, V. L. (2008). Seeking enlightenment on the dark side of psychology. *Trauma, Violence, and Abuse, 9*(2), 72–83. doi: 10.1177/1524838008314936. Retrieved from https:// web.archive.org/web/20150406210328/http:// www.queensu.ca/psychology/Quinsey/publications/Other/ darkside2008.pdf

Ray, D. W. (2009, May 11). *God Virus Part 8: The Sexual Guilt Cycle* [Video file]. Retrieved from http://www.youtube.com/watch? v=SLsNZ8vk1Xs

Regnerus, M., Price, J., & Gordon, D. (2017). Masturbation and partnered sex: Substitutes or complements? *Archives of Sexual Behavior, 46*(7), 2111– 2121. doi:10.1007/s10508-017-0975-8

Reichert, T. (2002). Sex in advertising research: A review of content, effects, and functions of sexual information in consumer advertising. *Annual Review of Sex Research, 13,* 241–273.

Rind, B., Tromovitch, P., & Bauserman, R. (1998). A meta-analytic examination of assumed properties of child sexual abuse using college samples. *Psychological Bulletin, 124*(1), 22–53. doi: 10.1037/0033-2909.124.1.22

Ronay, R., & von Hippel, W. (2010). The presence of an attractive woman elevates testosterone and physical risk-taking in young men. *Social Psychological and Personality Science, 1,* 57–64. doi: 10.1177/1948550609352807. Retrieved from https:// www2.psy.uq.edu.au/~uqwvonhi/R%26vH.SPPS.10.pdf

Roney, J. R. (2003). Effects of visual exposure to the opposite sex: Cognitive aspects of mate attraction in human males. *Personality and Social Psychology Bulletin, 29*(3), 393–404. doi: 10.1177/0146167202250221

Rosenblatt, A., Greenberg, J., Solomon, S., Pyszczynski, T., & Lyon, D. (1989). Evidence for terror management theory: I. The effects of mortality salience on reactions to those who violate or uphold cultural values. *Journal of Personality and Social Psychology, 57*(4), 681–690. doi: 10.1037/0022-3514.57.4.681

Rozée, P. D. (1993). Forbidden or forgiven? Rape in cross-cultural perspective. *Psychology of Women Quarterly, 17*(4), 499–514. doi:10.1111/j. 1471-6402.1993.tb00658.x

Sadler, A. G., Booth, B. M., Cook, B. L., & Doebbeling, B. N. (2003). Factors associated with women's risk of rape in the military environment. *American*

Journal of Industrial Medicine, 43(3), 262–273. doi:10.1002/ajim.10202

Sanday, P. R. (1981). The socio-cultural context of rape: A cross-cultural study. *Journal of Social Issues, 37*(4), 5–27. doi:10.1111/j.1540-4560.1981.tb01068.x

Savin-Williams, R. C. (2006). Who's gay? Does it matter? *Current Directions in Psychological Science, 15*(1), 40–44. doi:10.1111/j.0963-7214.2006.00403.x

Savin-Williams, R. C., Joyner, K., & Rieger, G. (2012). Prevalence and stability of self-reported sexual orientation identity during young adulthood. *Archives of Sexual Behavior, 41*(1), 103–110. doi:10.1007/s10508-012-9913-y

Schlegel, A., & Barry, H., III. (1987). The cultural consequences of female contribution to subsistence. *American Anthropologist, 88*(1), 142–150. Retrieved from http://www.jstor.org/stable/679286

Scorolli, C., Ghirlanda, S., Enquist, M., Zattoni, S., & Jannini, E. A. (2007). Relative prevalence of different fetishes. *International Journal of Impotence Research, 19*(4), 432–437. doi:10.1038/sj.ijir.3901547

Senn, C. Y., Desmarais, S., Verberg, N., & Wood, E. (2000). Predicting coercive sexual behavior across the lifespan in a random sample of Canadian men. *Journal of Social and Personal Relationships, 17*(1), 95–113. doi:10.1177/0265407500171005

Seto, M. C. (2008). *Pedophilia and sexual offending against children: Theory, assessment, and intervention.* Washington, DC: American Psychological Association. ISBN 978-1-4338-0114-3. doi:10.1037/11639-000

Seto, M. C. (2012). Is pedophilia a sexual orientation? *Archives of Sexual Behavior, 41*(1), 231–236. doi:10.1007/s10508-011-9882-6

Seto, M. C., & Lalumière, M. L. (2010). What is so special about male adolescent sexual offending? A review and test of explanations through meta-analysis. *Psychological Bulletin, 136*(4), 526–575. doi:10.1037/a0019700

Shan, W., Shenghua, J., Davis, H. M., Peng, K., Shao, X., Wu, Y., ... Wang, Y. (2012). Mating strategies in Chinese culture: Female risk avoiding vs. male risk taking. *Evolution and Human Behavior, 33*(3), 182–192. doi:10.1016/j.evolhumbehav.2011.09.001

Smith, D. (2005, May 17). A critic takes on the logic of female orgasm. *The New York Times.* Retrieved from http://www.nytimes.com/2005/05/17/science/17orga.html

Snowden, R. J., Wichter, J., & Gray, N. S. (2008). Implicit and explicit measurements of sexual preference in gay and heterosexual men: A comparison of priming techniques and the Implicit Association Task. *Archives of Sexual Behavior, 37*(4), 558–565. doi:10.1007/s10508-006-9138-z

Starin, E. D. (2004). Masturbation observations in Temmnick's red colobus. *Folia Primatologica, 75*(2), 114–117. doi:10.1159/000076273

Stearns, P. N. (2009). *Sexuality in world history.* London, England: Routledge. ISBN 0-203-88032-3.

Stevenson, R. J., Case, T. I., & Oaten, M. J. (2011). Effect of self-reported sexual arousal on responses to sex-related and non-sex-related disgust cues.

Archives of Sexual Behavior, 40(1), 79–85. doi:10.1007/
s10508-009-9529-z

Sullivan, J. (2005, July 15). Enumclaw-area animal-sex case investigated. *The Seattle Times.* Retrieved from http://www.seattletimes.com/
seattle-news/enumclaw-area-animal-sex-case-investigated

Tan, M., Jones, G., Zhu, G., Ye, J., Hong, T., Zhou, S., ... Zhang, L. (2009). Fellatio by fruit bats prolongs copulation time. *PLOS ONE.* doi:
10.1371/journal.pone.0007595

Taylor, L. D. (2012). Death and television: Terror management theory and themes of law and justice on television. *Death Studies, 36*(4), 340–359. doi:10.1080/07481187.2011.553343

Testa, M., & Dermen, K. H. (1999). The differential correlates of sexual coercion and rape. *Journal of Interpersonal Violence, 14*(5), 548–561. doi:10.1177/088626099014005006

Tharp, A. T., DeGue, S., Valle, L. A., Brookmeyer, K. A., Massetti, G. M., & Matjasko, J. L. (2013). A systematic qualitative review of risk and protective factors for sexual violence perpetration. *Trauma, Violence, and Abuse, 14*(2), 133–167. doi:10.1177/1524838012470031. Retrieved from http://www.researchgate.net/publication/234012107/
file/d912f51154c6ba4136.pdf

Thomsen, R., & Soltis, J. (2004). Male masturbation in free-ranging Japanese macaques. *International Journal of Primatology, 25*(5), 1033–1041. doi:
10.1023/B:IJOP.0000043350.75897.89

Toates, F. (2009). An integrative theoretical framework for understanding sexual motivation, arousal, and behavior. *Journal of Sex Research, 46*(2, 3), 168–193. doi:10.1080/00224490902747768

Tournaye, H., Staessen, C., Camus, M., Verheyen, G., Devroey, P., & Van Steirteghem, A. (1997). No evidence for a decreased fertilizing potential after in-vitro fertilization using spermatozoa from polyzoospermic men. *Human Reproduction, 12*(10), 2183–2185. doi:10.1093/humrep/
12.10.2183

Trost, J. E., & Bergstrom-Walan, M.-B. (2004). Sweden. In R. T. Francoeur & R. J. Noonan (Eds.), *The Continuum complete international encyclopedia of sexuality.* New York, NY: Continuum. Retrieved from https://
kinseyinstitute.org/pdf/ccies-sweden.pdf

Truman, J. L., & Planty, M. (2012). *Criminal victimization, 2011.* Washington, DC: US Department of Justice, Bureau of Justice Statistics. Retrieved from http://www.bjs.gov/content/pub/pdf/cv11.pdf

Tsunoda, Y., & Chang, M. C. (1975). Penetration of mouse eggs in vitro: Optimal sperm concentration and minimal number of spermatozoa. *Journal of Reproduction and Fertility, 44*(1), 139–142. doi:10.1530/jrf.
0.0440139

Van den Bergh, B., Dewitte, S., & Warlop, L. (2008). Bikinis instigate generalized impatience in intertemporal choice. *Journal of Consumer Research, 35*, 85–97. doi:10.1086/525505

Van Vugt, M., & Iredale, W. (2013). Men behaving nicely: Public goods as peacock tails. *British Journal of Psychology, 104*(1), 3–13. doi:10.1111/
j.2044-8295.2011.02093.x

Vandermassen, G. (2011). Evolution and rape: A feminist Darwinian perspective. *Sex Roles, 64*(9, 10), 732–747. doi:10.1007/s11199-010-9895-y

Vicary, J. R., Klingaman, L. R., & Harkness, W. L. (1995). Risk factors associated with date rape and sexual assault of adolescent girls. *Journal of Adolescence, 18*(3), 289–306. doi:10.1006/jado.1995.1020

Voller, E. K., Long, P. J., & Aosved, A. C. (2009). Attraction to sexual violence towards women, sexual abuse of children, and non-sexual criminal behavior: Testing the specialist vs. generalist models in male college students. *Archives of Sexual Behavior, 38*(2), 235–243. doi:10.1007/s10508-008-9343-z

Vrana, S., & Lauterbach, D. (1994). Prevalence of traumatic events and post-traumatic psychological symptoms in a nonclinical sample of college students. *Journal of Traumatic Stress, 7*(2), 289–302. doi:10.1002/jts.2490070209

Walton, M. T., Lykins, A. D., & Bhullar, N. (2016). Beyond heterosexual, bisexual, and homosexual: A diversity in sexual identity expression. *Archives of Sexual Behavior.* Advance online publication. doi:10.1007/s10508-016-0778-3

Waterman, J. M. (2010). The adaptive function of masturbation in a promiscuous African ground squirrel. *PLOS ONE.* doi:10.1371/journal.pone.0013060

Weinrich, J. D., Snyder, P. J., Pillard, R. C., Grant, I., Jacobson, D. L., Robinson, S. R., & McCutchan, J. A. (1993). A factor analysis of the Klein Sexual Orientation Grid in two disparate samples. *Archives of Sexual Behavior, 22*(2), 157–168. doi:10.1007/BF01542364

Whitaker, D. J., Le, B., Hanson, R. K., Baker, C. K., McMahon, P. M., Ryan, G., … Rice, D. D. (2008). Risk factors for the perpetration of child sexual abuse: A review and meta-analysis. *Child Abuse and Neglect, 32*(5), 529–548. doi:10.1016/j.chiabu.2007.08.005

Wilson, M., & Daly, M. (2004). Do pretty women inspire men to discount the future? *Proceedings of the Royal Society B, 271,* S177–S179. doi:10.1098/rsbl.2003.0134

Wilson, T. D., & Brekke, N. (1994). Mental contamination and mental correction: Unwanted influences on judgments and evaluations. *Psychological Bulletin, 116*(1), 117–142. doi:10.1037/0033-2909.116.1.117

Woolley, S. C., Sakata, J. T., & Crews, D. (2004). Tracing the evolution of brain and behavior using two related species of whiptail lizards: *Cnemidophorus uniparens* and *Cnemidophorus inornatus. ILAR Journal, 45*(1), 46–53. Retrieved from https://web.archive.org/web/20120904060605/http://dels-old.nas.edu/ilar_n/ilarjournal/45_1/pdfs/v4501woolley.pdf

Yalom, I. D. (1980). *Existential psychotherapy.* New York, NY: Basic Books. ISBN 0465021476.

Young, S. D., & Jordan, A. H. (2013). The influence of social networking photos on social norms and sexual health behaviors. *Cyberpsychology, Behavior, and Social Networking, 16*(4), 243–247. doi:10.1089/cyber.2012.0080

Yu, C. K.-C. (2012). Pornography consumption and sexual behaviors as correlates of erotic dreams and nocturnal emissions. *Dreaming, 22*(4), 230–239. doi:10.1037/a0030254

Yule, M. A., Brotto, L. A., & Gorzalka, B. B. (2015). A validated measure of no sexual attraction: The Asexuality Identification Scale. *Psychological Assessment, 27*(1), 148–160. doi:10.1037/a0038196

Zamboni, B. D., & Crawford, I. (2002). Using masturbation in sex therapy: Relationships between masturbation, sexual desire, and sexual fantasy. *Journal of Psychology and Human Sexuality, 14*(2, 3), 123–141. doi:10.1300/J056v14n02_08

www.ingramcontent.com/pod-product-compliance
Lightning Source LLC
Chambersburg PA
CBHW072207280526
45788CB00002B/913